The Instant Guide to Healthy
Windowbox & Balcony Plants

Series editor: David Longman

Colour illustrations by Andrew Riley, Jane Pickering and Bob Bampton

The Instant Guide to Healthy
Windowbox
& Balcony Plants

Norman
Simpson

Times
BOOKS

THE AUTHOR

Norman Simpson has had many years of practical horticultural
experience, first from helping on his parents' smallholding (which
specialized in cut flowers), then from building up and running his
own nursery. He is now manager of Asmer Seeds Trials and
Research Centre at Syston in Leicestershire, England, where
emphasis is placed on the selection and breeding of plants from
seed.

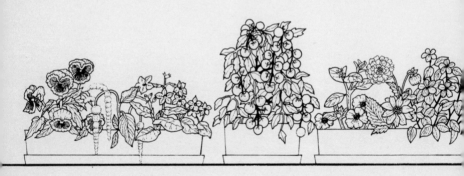

Originally published in Great Britain in 1984 as *How to Care for
Your Windowbox and Balcony Plants* by Peter Lowe, London.

Library of Congress Catalog Card Number: 84-40638
International Standard Book Number: 0-8129-1178-4

Printed in Italy by Amilcare Pizzi SpA

987654321
First American Edition

Contents

Common names

Scientific names

Introduction

How to use this book

Urban areas are crowded with buildings and few large gardens exist within them. To improve the quality of one's surroundings is a recognized human need and growing plants is an effective and economical way of doing it. Indoor plants are dealt with in other volumes in this comprehensive series; outdoors in a city the windowbox, patio tub or balcony container is often the only place where growing plants can be kept.

Almost any plant can be grown in a container: the list provided in this book is a selection that contains some shrubs, fruits, annuals and perennials, all of which can be propagated by an amateur gardener.

Each two-page spread is devoted to a single species of plant. The left-hand page describes the plant and explains how to look after it, giving the correct amount of water, light and feeding it requires. Little can be done to control temperature on balconies and windowsills but where protection from frost, hot sun or bad weather is needed, this is specified. There is also a list of suitable varieties and a colour photo of a healthy plant. On the right-hand page is a colour painting of the plant showing all the things that can go wrong with it. Since it shows all these problems at once, it may understandably look rather odd. The caption beside each symptom tells you what is wrong at that point and explains how to put it right.

Many of the plants suggested are annual flowering ones, which grow from seed, flower and die in a single season. These quickly provide a colourful display and give you a chance to experiment before committing yourself to a long-term planting scheme – in which they can still feature.

Finally, the pests, diseases and other problems shown in the paintings are not inevitable so do not be deterred by a seemingly endless catalogue of troubles. With the minimum of correct care and attention healthy plants will grow and bloom, bringing life and colour to the dullest city street.

Tools for container gardening

It is possible to look after plants with very little equipment but if you intend to grow from seed and care for plants from year to year, it is well worth investing in some good quality tools.

Keep separate sprayers and watering cans for insecticides and fungicides and a stock of basic chemicals. Do not buy in large quantities. Mark all containers used for chemicals clearly and wash them out regularly. Always check the labels before use.

For seed growing, use seed trays for germination and for pricking out seedlings. Peat pots are also useful for individual sowing. A propagator conserves moisture and heated models give bottom heat for seeds and cuttings. A thermometer and moisture meter are useful.

6

A good trowel is a must for planting and a small fork is useful for weeding. A small spade or shovel helps to mix compost well and to fill larger containers. A plastic bucket can be used for mixing composts.

Keep a supply of both seed and potting composts. Some plants require lime-free mixtures. Sharp sand can be obtained from garden centres. Fertilizer, hormone rooting powder (for cuttings) and charcoal (for hanging baskets) are all useful.

Wear gloves to protect your hands. Secateurs, scissors and a sharp knife are useful for tidying and taking cuttings.

A watering can to which a rose can be attached is essential. Never use your normal watering can for chemicals.

Containers come in all shapes and sizes and may be plastic, stone or wood. Make sure they have drainage holes. Broken crocks make good drainage material. Canes, twine, raffia and plant rings are useful for training. Hessian or sacking is useful for protection in cold climates.

Containers

Any container that will hold soil and allow surplus water to drain away freely can be used but as plants are grown to improve the environment, the container should not detract from that by being ugly or unsightly. Natural hewn stone, reconstituted stone or hardwoods are ideal but the plastics industry has made great strides in producing classical designs cheaply and these are now made with more natural effect than the stark white urns of a few years ago. Even these can be improved by painting them with a natural stone finish though the surface must be well roughened with glass paper first or the paint will soon flake. Hand-thrown pottery containers, both glazed and unglazed, are also attractive.

Old sinks, halved beer barrels, old garden wheelbarrows are also much used for planting. Windowboxes may be in wood, plastic or concrete and often come with the house so that no choice is possible. Whatever is used, the judicious use of trailing plants can do much to hide the stark outlines.

Always secure windowboxes carefully and make sure that pots or tubs on sills or balconies are stable. A container full of soil and plants can cause considerable damage if it falls down.

The compost

The formula for a standard compost was devised many years ago by the John Innes Institute for Horticultural Research and was designed to provide a sterile medium suitable for a wide range of plants. Good loamy soil was an essential part of this formula and this has become more difficult to obtain recently, resulting in variations in quality, despite apparently identical ingredients. Loam-based compost is usually sold with fertilizer added, the numbers 1,2, and 3 indicating the different proportions used. In this book the compost is referred to as 'loam-based No. 1, 2, or 3' with 3 the richest and 1 the weakest in added fertilizer.

Loamless composts, based on peat, were first devised by the University of California

Preparing a container

1. Treat wooden containers inside and out with wood preservative before using.

2. If using a light plastic urn or pot with a hollow base, pack hollow with plastic bag filled with sand to make it more stable. Choose wide-based containers where possible.

3. Make sure container has drainage holes and raise base off floor with tiles or bricks. This ensures free drainage and helps to keep pests away.

4. Place layer of stones, broken clay pots or crocks to cover base of container. Sterilize them first with solution of permanganate of potash. Crocks should be at least 1in (2½cm) deep. If no drainage holes, crocks should take up ¼ depth of container.

5. Add layer of pea gravel or very small pebbles on top of crocks.

6. Fill with compost, leaving about 2in (5cm) at top to allow for watering. Water well and leave to drain for at least 2 hours before planting. If compost settles after watering, top up with fresh.

Sowing the seed

1. Fill seed tray to rim with seedling compost, using slight pressure only at corners.

2. Press down very lightly with flat board so surface is flat and even.

3. Water through a fine rose until it comes through bottom of tray. Leave to drain for at least 2 hours.

4. Always sow seed thinly. Large seeds can be spaced individually as instructed on packet.

5. Cover them with fresh dry seedling compost so seed is just hidden.

6. For very fine seed (e.g. Begonia), mix it with 20 times its volume of fine dry sand.

7. Place mixture on palm of hand, open palm fully and tap side of palm with index finger of other hand. The mixture will move to edge of palm and drop a few grains at a time onto compost. Move hand slowly above tray so seed is sown evenly and well spaced. Do not cover fine seed.

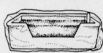

8. Do not water but insert label with date and name and place tray in propagator or plastic bag with end folded under tray to conserve moisture.

9. Check temperature and light requirements for each plant. Cover with brown paper if necessary and keep in even temperature, away from windows.

10. Move into light place, remove covering as soon as seeds begin to grow.

---

and have largely taken the place of John Innes for propagating purposes, being clean, light and easily handled. They are very uniform and any problems that arise in use are likely to be due to poor storage conditions. The moisture content of the peat must be exactly right at the time of mixing. If the bag is stored outside, inevitably the compost will become wetter and this will activate the slow release fertilizers and give rise to a compost that is too strong for young seedlings. So keep your compost under cover and out of the sun which will also cause slight chemical changes that may be harmful. The expense of any prepacked compost is in its sterility: do not waste money by mixing it with unsterilized soil, putting it in dirty seed trays or watering it with contaminated water.

An even more recent development is rockwool as a growing medium but its use at present is highly scientific and unsuitable for ordinary gardening.

Sowing the seed

Few people have a heated greenhouse in which to propagate but by following the instructions in this book, excellent plants can be raised ready for planting in early summer and at little cost on the sill of a sunny, light window indoors.

The basic preparation is common to all seed sowing (see above), while any special requirements are given under individual plant entries. The best germinating temperature is also given there for each subject. Clean trays, sterile seedling compost and clean tap water are the main essentials.

Small, lightweight plastic seed trays or pots are ideal for sowing and are more sterile than wood. Plastic pots will be needed for sowing, taking cuttings and potting on. The most useful sizes are 3in (8cm), 3½in (9cm), 4¼ (11cm) and 5½in (14cm). Cut flat presser bonds from thin hardboard to fit the tray size, adding a small block of wood as a handle. Keep a small airtight jar full of dry, fine sand for mixing with fine seed: to get the sand really fine, pass it through an old nylon stocking.

A heated propagator is useful but a plastic bag wrapped around the tray makes a good substitute as long as the trays can be kept in a warm, even temperature. Most seed will germinate in half light and a brown paper cover will provide this. Once germinated, the seedlings can be kept on a windowledge with double glazing or protected from draughts by a sheet of plastic. Always label seed when sown so that progress can be checked from the date on the label.

Pricking out

As soon as the first signs of growth are seen, remove the tray from its plastic bag or propagator into a light position, though not in scorching sun. It is important to prick out (transplant) the seedlings into a tray or pot of fresh compost as soon as they are large enough to handle; the seedling will then hardly be aware that it has been moved. In the case of French marigolds and other rapidly germinating seeds this can be as early as 6 days after sowing. Pricking out allows the seedling more room for its roots to develop and, if properly spaced, the plant can be left in this pot or tray until planted outside in its final container.

Hardening off

This is a difficult thing to get right and some explanation of the term is necessary first. Some plants are termed hardy. These will withstand winter frosts and burst into growth again in the spring. Some are half hardy and these in general comprise plants which will grow out-of-doors in the summer but will be killed by any frost. 'Tender' plants are particularly affected by cold

weather and must be treated with special care. But all this has nothing to do with hardening off. Any plant introduced to the outside world from a protected indoor environment will receive a shock to its system. The art is to minimize this shock by making the introduction as gradual as possible. This process is known as hardening off. If correctly hardened off, hardy plants will still survive the winter and half hardy plants will still be killed by frost; but neither of them will be needlessly damaged by chills and shock.

Young plants are normally taken outside in mid to late spring. For the first week they should be covered with glass or plastic to allow them to adjust to cooler temperatures. If you have no cold frame, line a small crate with plastic and cover it with a sheet of glass. Air is allowed in during the day, but the cover is closed at night. At first the air may only be allowed in for 2 hours a day but after 2 to 3 days the cover can be taken off completely during fine weather. If frost is expected at night, the frame should be covered and wrapped in hessian if the plants it contains are half hardy and even for hardy ones during their first week outside. Remove the cover early in the morning or condensation will not dry off before the sun is hot and the leaves will be scorched. Late uncovering also means lost light and this is important to keep the plants growing sturdily. Half hardy plants need at least 14 days to harden off sufficiently to withstand the effects of cold spring winds, but protection must at any rate continue until all risk of frost is passed. Bought plants should be ready for planting out but if purchased early in the season, check whether they are tender or hardy before leaving out unprotected. If in doubt, cover plants with an inverted cardboard box wrapped in newspapers, sacking and polythene on frosty nights.

One important final point. Wet protection is worse than no protection. Cover frost wraps with plastic sheet. Leaves should be dry before the frame is closed for the night. The whole spring effort of germinating and

Pricking out

Seedlings should be pricked out as soon as they are large enough to handle.

1. You will need a tray, small pots or peat pots of fresh seedling compost and a dibber or blunt-ended stick for making flat-bottomed holes. Or, drill a flat board with ¼in (6mm) holes 2in (5cm) apart and glue blunt-ended pegs about 1in (2½cm) long in position to make several holes at once.

2. Water compost and leave to drain for 2 hours.

3. Make flat-bottomed holes 2in (5cm) apart, about 1in (2½cm) deep in compost.

4. Push plant label or ice lolly stick into compost in tray of seedlings and spoon up 3 or 4.

5. Place in palm of hand and, holding by leaves, take them 1 by 1 in other hand and drop them into holes in new tray or pots. Do not press compost around stems.

6. Water with tap water using fine rosed can and put in shady place for 2 days. Compost should be just moist so that roots grow in search of water. Keep seedlings in a light, draught-free place until ready for planting out. Check individual light and temperature needs.

growing, the whole summer's pleasure, can be lost in one night without this care.

In cold climates, frost will completely freeze the soil in containers in winter. Wrap them in sacking and cover with a polythene sheet to keep them dry.

Watering and spraying

Most plants will stay healthy in a moist soil, that is one that retains all the water its solid particles can hold without filling the air spaces that are so essential to the roots. In the garden, excess water can seep away over a wide area but in a container drainage holes are necessary to allow any excess to drain quickly after watering so that air can take its place. Without proper drainage, the soil soon becomes waterlogged and even moisture-loving plants will suffer and eventually die. Some plants are sensitive to even a short period without air at their roots and for these you are instructed to keep them 'on the dry side' but don't make the mistake of keeping them completely dry. Instead, allow the soil to dry out almost to the bottom of the container between waterings.

For many years the water butt was considered essential to good gardening but unless it is kept scrupulously sterile – no easy task – its water is quite unsuitable for seedlings. It is certain to contain disease organisms which will thrive in the warm, humid conditions of a propagator. Tap water is safe for propagation but if your container is planted with lime-hating species, it may contain too much calcium. For them sterilized rainwater is best.

Overwatering and contaminated water are the prime causes of failure of container-grown plants. Under individual plant entries you will find each plant's moisture preference but it is virtually impossible to recommend watering intervals outside, where rainfall and temperature radically affect the rate at which a container dries out. It is best to test the soil regularly (especially for windowboxes, which may be sheltered from the rain) and to watch carefully for any signs of drooping leaves or flowers.

Many plants enjoy an overhead spray and this will be especially welcome to plants growing under an overhanging balcony where rain does not normally reach; plants with soft stems and leaves are likely to develop botrytis mould if they are regularly wetted and these, of course, should not be sprayed. Again, individual requirements are given in the plant entries.

Feeding

Container-grown plants need more regular feeding than garden plants because each time you water the container the nutrients are washed down further and further until they have all disappeared through the drainage holes. In the garden the roots can still reach them. Soil-based composts retain these nutrients for longer than soil-less ones and it is for this reason that different feeding rates are recommended for each. Liquid fertilizers are instantly available to the roots but must always be diluted to at least the maker's recommended strength. There are also a number of slow-release tabs, sticks and granules available and these can be a useful standby, especially when plants are left for some time unattended.

In general, start feeding seed-grown plants 3–4 weeks after planting out. Never feed dry plants. Always water them first and allow to drain for an hour or so before feeding. Never think that a double dose will be twice as good as one: it will scorch the roots. Foliar feeds, sprayed on the leaves, are beneficial, but use them with care: dilute to the recommended strength and do not spray in bright sunshine.

When buying fertilizer, choose a balanced mixture of nitrogen and potash never all potash or all nitrogen or the plant's delicate balance will be upset. Potash provides colour, firmness of foliage and disease resistance. Nitrogen gives quicker growth and greenness of leaf.

Using chemicals

In recent years many of the insects and animals which controlled pests have disappeared as their habitats have been destroyed and, without natural enemies, garden pests have increased. Chemical control is often the only weapon available but the general principal should be that if a pest can be destroyed by hand picking, rubbing or washing off, then this should be done. If chemicals have to be resorted to, they should always be used with great care, following the maker's instructions and the rules set out on page 13.

Planting a mixed container

1. Prepare container and assemble plants ready to be transferred. Water plants well.

2. Dig small holes with trowel where plants are to go. These should be large enough to take whole root ball. Leave plenty of space for growth.

3. Insert canes if needed for tall or climbing plants, to avoid damaging roots later on.

4. Remove plant carefully from pot or tray, disturbing root ball and soil as little as possible. For pots, knock edge and hold hand over soil while removing plant.

5. For trays, knock side and tilt whole tray forward to loosen plants, holding hand over them to prevent them falling out completely.

6. Put larger plants in position first. Do not plant too deep. They should be at same level as before. Deeper planting encourages root rot.

7. Peat pots can be planted whole. The plant's roots will grow through them.

8. Firm compost gently around plant and continue transferring in order of size until container is complete.

9. Fill any spaces with small plants to give an even look but remember to leave room for growth. Do not water for 2 days.

10. Start feeding 3–4 weeks after planting container. Feed evenly over whole soil. If feed gets on leaves, wash it off with clean water to prevent scorching.

Fungicides: *Benomyl.* Moderately safe. Can irritate throat. *Bordeaux mixture.* Moderately safe unless swallowed. *Cheshunt compound.* Moderately safe unless swallowed. Do not smell. *Dinocap.* May irritate skin, eyes, nose, mouth. Wear mask and goggles. *Iprodione.* May irritate nose and throat. Harmful to fish.

Insecticides and pesticides: *Derris.* Plant derived, controls aphids, helps with red spider mite, caterpillar, thrips. Relatively safe for humans, toxic to fish. *Dimethoate.* Controls red spider and aphid. Dangerous to humans and animals. *Gamma-BHC (or HCH).* Kills earwigs, cutworm, caterpillars, leatherjackets. Toxic if inhaled. Taints food crops and persists in soil for many years. *Malathion.* Controls wide range of pests. Toxic to some plants, harmful to humans, bees, fish. *Metaldehyde.* Controls slugs and snails. Harmful if swallowed to humans, animals, fish, birds. Used in slug pellets. *Pirimicarb.* Kills aphid only. Safe.

Months and seasons

The plants in this book are suitable for a wide range of climates. To make the instructions useful for as many areas as possible, dates are given in seasons not months. The following chart gives the monthly equivalents.

Month in northern hemisphere	Season	Month in southern hemisphere
January	**Mid-Winter**	July
February	**Late Winter**	August
March	**Early Spring**	September
April	**Mid-Spring**	October
May	**Late Spring**	November
June	**Early Summer**	December
July	**Mid-Summer**	January
August	**Late Summer**	February
September	**Early Autumn**	March
October	**Mid-Autumn**	April
November	**Late Autumn**	May
December	**Early Winter**	June

Taking care with chemicals

Many chemicals are poisonous. Use them with respect.

Never handle an open bottle of concentrate without gloves.

Never smell or breathe in sprays or dusts.

Never mix different types of insecticides as the chemicals may react.

Never put them into other bottles, such as soft drink or beer bottles.

Never spray in windy weather.

Never spray when bees are visiting flowers.

Never pour them down the sink or drains. Do not even pour the water in which you have washed containers and sprayers down the drain.

Never make up more at one time than you will use.

Never keep diluted insecticide for more than 24 hours.

Never leave old containers or unused contents of watering cans lying around.

Never eat, smoke or drink without first washing your hands.

Always follow instructions carefully. Do not over or under dilute.

Always use a separate watering can and sprayer, keeping another one for normal spraying and watering.

Always keep nozzle of spray at least 12in (30cm) from leaves.

Always spray in the evening, in still weather.

Always keep away from fishponds and pets. Some chemicals taint food crops.

Always keep away from food and food/drink containers.

Always store them with their sprayers and containers in a dry, frost-free place, on a high shelf out of reach of children.

Always wash out all sprayers and empty bottles after use, inside and out.

Always pour washing water onto ground away from food crops and water sources such as streams and rivers.

Always throw empty bottles and containers away with domestic waste.

Always wash thoroughly in hot water and detergent when you have used them.

Ageratum

Ageratum is deservedly popular as a neat, continuous flowering annual. Modern hybrids rarely exceed 6in (15cm) and so are ideal for window-boxes or around the edge of a large patio or balcony tub. They are prone to fungus diseases and the best way to keep them healthy and ensure they grow bushily is to transfer them from seed tray to container as soon as they are large enough to handle.

Light: Indoors, maximum. Outdoors, no more than 2 hours shade.
Temperature: Germination, 65–70°F (18–21°C). Just before planting outdoors, 45°F (7°C). Protect from frost.
Water: Moist compost. Underwater rather than overwater. Protect from heavy rain.
Humidity: Do not syringe, spray or water overhead when in flower.
Soil: Loam-based No. 2, or soil-less potting compost. It must be completely sterile.
Feeding: Feed regularly to keep the plants growing. Feed young seedlings with half-strength liquid fertilizer. Ten days after final planting start feeding at full recom-mended strength. Repeat every 10 days for soil-based, every 5 days for soil-less compost.
Propagation: Prepare tray in early spring. Sow seed but do not cover with compost. Place in propagator case or plastic bag giv-ing 70°F (21°C) bottom heat. Germination occurs within 1 week. Prick out seedlings 2in (5cm) apart as soon as they are large enough to handle. Keep at 65°C (18°C) for 1 week. Cool gradually down to 45°F (7°C) just before planting out.
Tidying: Cut off any flowers which turn brown with age. Cut at base of stem.
Varieties: Blue Mink, powder blue (6in, 15cm). Blue Danube, bright blue, dwarf, compact and early. Spindrift, white, com-pact and early.

Ageratums are between 4–18in (10–45cm) tall, with broad, bright green oval leaves which are slightly rough to the touch. The fluffy flowers are massed together on each stem and are usually lavender blue with more rarely white, pink and deep blue varieties.

Flower heads turn brown. Insecticide or fertilizer too strong, insecticide sprayed in sunlight, or cat damage. Always use correct dilution of feed and chemicals. Do not spray in sunlight.

Leaves turn grey/green and plant droops in sun. Too dry. Water well, allow to drain until just moist before watering again.

Newly emerged seedlings collapse; stems thread-like near soil. Pythium fungus. If time, sow again in sterile compost and water only with tap water. If only some affected, plant out only those well away from affected area.

Whole plant collapses, eaten at soil level. Cutworm or woodlice. Search top inch (2½cm) of compost for cutworm (unlikely in sterilized compost). Dust with gamma BHC or destroy woodlice by hand.

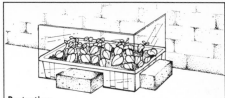

Protection

Young plants hardening off outside should be shielded from cold winds. If no cold frame available, position sheets of glass on windward side, holding in place with bricks.

Small spots on leaves. Leaf-spotting fungus. Spray with Bordeaux mixture at recommended strength every 10 days until clear.

Growing point distorted and covered in tiny insects. Aphids. Spray with pirimicarb at recommended strength. Repeat after 1 week if pest returns.

what goes wrong

Plant droops, flowers lose fluffiness. Water on leaves and flowers. Do not spray or water overhead.

Holes in leaves, growing points eaten. Slug damage. Put down recommended slug bait around plant base.

Leaves of mature plant eaten. Caterpillar damage. Pick off pest or dust with gamma BHC or derris.

Plant turns black and soggy in late spring/early autumn. Frost. Protect whenever frost expected.

Leaves of young plants turn brown or bronzed. Cold winds or put outside too soon. Protect from wind.

Leaves hang down, soil dark and slimy. Waterlogged. Overwatered or badly drained. Clear drainage holes and do not water again until surface dries out.

Leaves of young plants grey and soggy. Botrytis, from wet soil and little air movement. Spray with benomyl or iprodione.

15

Amaranthus caudatus

Love lies bleeding

Loves lies bleeding is a native of India but survives well in temperate climates. Its name comes from the long, rather sad-looking tassels, whose tiny flowers open progressively as the stem gets longer and are much loved by bees. From a rather weedy start, it becomes very robust as the season progresses and will, therefore, need plenty of room in a mixed container or it will hide some of its smaller companions. An annual, it will be killed by frost at the end of the summer.

Light: Maximum.
Temperature: Will survive cold but not frost, and prefers warm summers, 70°F (21°C) or more.
Water: Little and often so that the soil is always just moist. Must be well drained.
Humidity: Spraying unnecessary. It is not much affected by rain, but prefers dry weather.
Soil: Loam-based No. 2. Grows well in soilless compost but needs a mixture of about 50% soil to support its heavy top growth.
Feeding: Liquid feed every 10 days at maker's recommended strength.
Propagation: For sowing outdoors, water compost in container 24 hours before sowing in mid to end spring. Sow 2–3 seeds in groups about 12in (30cm) apart and cover with compost until just hidden. One week after seedlings appear, thin out leaving strongest in each group. Indoors, sow very thinly on surface of well-drained compost in a 3½in (9cm) pot. When seedlings are big enough to handle, plant them singly in 3½in (9cm) pots or 2in (5cm) apart in a tray.
Tidying: Remove any yellowing leaves at the base of the plant weekly.
Varieties: Some different coloured spikes, including a dirty white are available.

Love lies bleeding grows to 2–3ft (60–90cm) if the seed ha germinated indoors, less if sown outdoors. The leaves are mid-green with a red rib and have an elongated heart shape The tiny carmine coloured flowers are clustered along a growing, willowy stem, forming long tassels which may reach the ground.

Growing point distorted and does not grow well. Aphids. Spray with liquid derris or systemic insecticide to maker's instructions. Repeat after 10 days if symptoms persist.

what goes wrong

Mature leaves have dull red markings. Caused by cold. Move to more protected position if possible.

Growing point lopsided. Capsid bug damage. A dark spot surrounded by sunken area shows where bug has attacked stem. Drench with systemic insecticide diluted as maker recommends.

Leaves hard with bronze colour. Too much cold wind. Protect from prevailing wind.

Whole plant starts to become yellow and sickly. Too wet, waterlogged soil. Check drainage holes are clear and allow soil to dry out before watering again.

Plant blackened and limp. Frost damage. Protect from late spring frosts. Remove dead plant from container and sow more seed.

Plant collapses, leaves turn brown. Fed with too strong a mixture, roots burned. Plant may die, but do not feed for a month, then use half-strength mixture.

Holes on edges of leaves, especially at plant base. Slugs or snails, which are partial to this plant. Sprinkle slug pellets around base but make sure these cannot get into fish ponds.

Plant wilts. Too dry. Water immediately, then keep soil always moist but not waterlogged.

Seedlings grow tall and weedy, then collapse. Too dark. Keep in good light at all times.

Leaves turn brittle with pinky grey, mealy undersides. Red spider mite. Spray with diluted malathion every 14 days until clear.

Leaves turn yellow from base of plant. Needs feeding. Feed with liquid feed every 10 days, diluting according to maker's instructions.

17

Aucuba japonica

Spotted laurel

Unlike many plants in this book, Spotted laurels thrive in dappled or even heavy shade so are very useful for a shady corner. They will not, however, stand much frost and should be moved to a protected position if frosts are severe or prolonged. Buy berried plants in spring so that they have a chance to adapt to the outside during summer. For a good show of berries ask your nurseryman for 1 plant of each sex and pollinate by hand, transferring pollen with a camel hair paintbrush from the male flowers (with stamens) to the female (without).

Light: Mottled shade is ideal. Full shade or 1–2 hours of sun will be tolerated.

Temperature: Protect from cold, continuous wind and heavy frost.

Water: Needs plenty of water to keep always moist. Make sure drainage is good before planting in final container.

Humidity: Spray heavily in summer or sponge leaves to remove dirt.

Soil: Good quality loamy compost, such as loam-based No. 3.

Feeding: Plants are improved by regular feeding. Feed every 14 days, varying the feed between dry and liquid fertilizer. For first 3 months use half maker's recommended strength. Feed only from spring to autumn.

Propagation: Cuttings strike easily (see p.19) but will take a year or two to make a good sized plant. Keep in frost-free place for at least 1 year.

Tidying: Remove dead or yellow leaves. Prune only to keep a good shape, cutting back to just above a leaf joint.

Varieties: Picturata, attractive variegation (48in, 130cm). Variegata, good colour, likes some sunshine (60in, 160cm). Japonica, plain green, strong growing (72in, 2m).

Spotted laurels grow eventually to 10ft (3m) tall but take many years to reach this size. They have a dark woody base with paler stems and their evergreen leaves with yellow markings are about 6in (15cm) long. Small purple flowers in upright clusters are followed by oval red berries.

Leaves lose brightness, green dull. Wind scorch, too much sun or needs feeding. Check conditions. Protect from strong winds or move to more shady position. Feed every 14 days in spring and summer. If already feeding regularly, feed more often but not with stronger food.

Large brown areas on leaf edges. Fungal disease. Spray with iprodione.

Leaves lose variegated markings. Too dark. Move to lighter place.

All leaves turn brown, dry and dead. Severe frost. Plant will not survive prolonged frost so move container to sheltered area in hard winters.

Holes in centre and edges of leaves. Caterpillar. Pick off all pests or cocoons fastened to wall or window ledge. Spray with diluted malathion.

what goes wrong

Small brown scales on undersides of leaves. Oleander scale. Wipe off with cotton-wool dipped in methylated spirits. They increase in warm conditions. Check plant when buying to make sure it is clean.

Taking cuttings

1. In early summer choose stem with no berries or flowers and cut off 6in (15cm) from tip. Include 2 pairs leaves.

2. Trim just below lowest leaf. Remove lowest leaf. Dip cut end in hormone rooting powder.

3. Prepare small pot with drainage and seedling compost. Insert cutting so soil is level with lowest leaf. Place in shade indoors or in cold frame.

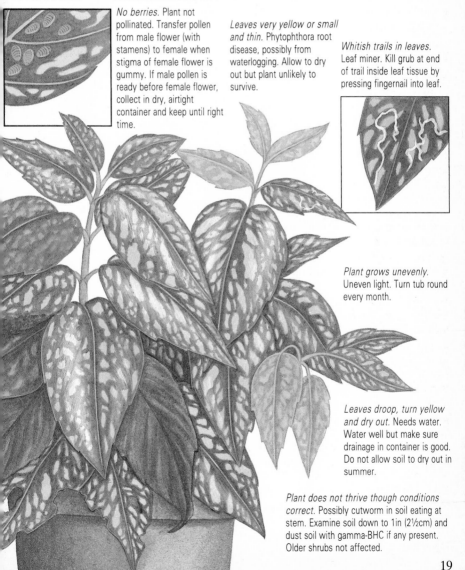

No berries. Plant not pollinated. Transfer pollen from male flower (with stamens) to female when stigma of female flower is gummy. If male pollen is ready before female flower, collect in dry, airtight container and keep until right time.

Leaves very yellow or small and thin. Phytophthora root disease, possibly from waterlogging. Allow to dry out but plant unlikely to survive.

Whitish trails in leaves. Leaf miner. Kill grub at end of trail inside leaf tissue by pressing fingernail into leaf.

Plant grows unevenly. Uneven light. Turn tub round every month.

Leaves droop, turn yellow and dry out. Needs water. Water well but make sure drainage in container is good. Do not allow soil to dry out in summer.

Plant does not thrive though conditions correct. Possibly cutworm in soil eating at stem. Examine soil down to 1in (2½cm) and dust soil with gamma-BHC if any present. Older shrubs not affected.

Begonia

The fibrous-rooted begonia is one of the most accommodating of all flowering plants. It can be raised from seed or from cuttings, is normally flowering by the time it is planted out and, if lifted and potted up before the frost, will continue to flower in the home until mid-winter. After being cut back and given a short rest period, it will begin flowering again in early spring. At its best in dappled sunlight, it will grow in most situations from full sun to shade but, being of Brazilian origin, will not stand frosts.

Light: Seedlings, good light but not full sun. Plants, full sun if well watered. They will take quite deep shade but prefer dappled sunlight.

Temperature: Germination, 70–75°F (23°C). Seedlings, 60°F (16°C). Lower indoor temperature gradually to 45°F (7°C) 3 weeks before planting out. No frost.

Water: The soil must neither be dry nor waterlogged. Keep always moist, especially in first 4 weeks from seed.

Humidity: A light overhead spray during spring to early autumn.

Soil: Loam-based No. 2 but a soil-less compost is better.

Feeding: Use liquid fertilizer diluted to half maker's recommended strength, every third watering.

Propagation: From seed (see p.21) or cuttings. Take cuttings 2in (5cm) long from last season's plant. Insert in seedling compost round outside of a 3½in (9cm) pot. Keep moist. They root in 3–4 weeks.

Tidying: Pick off fallen flowers from foliage.

Varieties: Pink Avalanche, Organdy Mixture, Danica Rose or Scarlet, large flowered and tall and all the Ambra series of colours.

These begonias grow to 6–10in (15–25cm) high, with fleshy stems and leaves which vary in colour from bright green to deep mahogany and have a glossy surface with a slightly duller underside. The colour range is limited to white, pink and red – but there are many variations of shade.

what goes wrong

Leaves turn brown at edges. If seedlings indoors, too much sun – move to more shady place. If just moved outside, cold winds. Keep young plants cool (45°F, 7°C) for 3 weeks before planting out to acclimatize them.

Leaves lose natural gloss and are dull and grey. Too dry. Increase watering. Brightness will return but will take some days. Do not overwater if they still look dull next day.

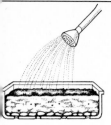

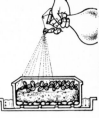

Propagation

1. Sow seed in spring, when days start to lengthen. Prepare seed tray with seedling compost and water well. Leave to drain for 2 hours.

2. Mix seed with 20 times its volume of fine sand, and sow onto surface of tray. Do not cover with compost. To sow evenly, hold seed mixture on palm of hand and tap edge of hand with index finger.

3. Place tray in plastic bag, and seal or put into propagator case. Cover with thick paper and leave at 70–75°F (21–24°C) for 10 days. When seedlings appear, remove paper but leave tray in unsealed bag in shade for 1 week.

4. If seedlings need water in first 2 weeks place tray in shallow water and mist spray daily. Later, water overhead. Prick out when large enough to handle.

New leaves pale, flowers small. Needs feeding. Feed with liquid fertilizer at half maker's recommended strength with every third watering.

Fluffy grey mould in centre of plant. Botrytis. If seedlings, give more air. Spray with benomyl and repeat in 10 days.

White powdery deposit on stems and patches on leaves. Powdery mildew. Spray with fungicide to maker's instructions and repeat every 10 days until clear.

Leaves yellow along veins. Wilt disease. Destroy plant and treat surrounding soil with cheshunt compound. Do not take cuttings from affected plant.

Plant turns yellow from base, whole plant does not thrive. Soil dark and scummy. Overwatered. Stop watering until soil nearly dry. If still wet after 2–3 days without water check drainage in container.

Leaves are blackened and droop. Frost damage. Begonias are tender. Protect from frost at all times.

Seedlings grow matted and intertwined, leaves and roots damaged when pricking out. Sown too thickly. Mix the extra-fine seed with 20 times its volume of very fine sand before sowing.

Browallia

This beautiful South American plant makes a magnificent display in a tub, hanging basket, trough or pot, providing it is not in a windy or draughty place. It can be raised from seed indoors in spring but should only be introduced gradually to the outside, when all danger of frost has passed. The first autumn frosts will kill it. It is sometimes grown as an indoor flowering pot plant.

Light: Indoors maximum but not direct sun. Outside, dappled sunlight: place taller plants or trellis between plant and sun. Full sun bleaches flowers and dries out plant.

Temperature: 55–70°F (13–21°C). Higher if well shaded. No frost.

Water: Good drainage and keep moist. It soon droops when dry.

Humidity: Regular syringing, 3 times a day in hottest summer days. Midday spraying safe if in shade and not already drooping.

Soil: Loam-based No. 1 or peat-based potting compost.

Feeding: Liquid feed at maker's recommended strength every 10 days in loam, every 5 in peat.

Propagation: In mid-spring, fill 3½in (9cm) pot with soil-less seedling compost pressed very lightly to make level surface. Water and drain for 2 hours. Sow seed very thinly and dust over with compost. Place in plastic bag or propagator at 55–65°F (13–18°C). Germination takes 7–10 days. Uncover and bring to light (not full sun). Prick off individually into 3in (5cm) pots as soon as big enough to handle. Water very lightly to settle soil around roots. Keep in airy room until all frost is passed. Then plant out.

Tidying: Remove yellowing leaves. Remove dead flowers which may go mouldy.

Varieties: Heavenly Bells, Blue Troll (dwarf), White Troll (dwarf).

Browallia is a tender annual which grows to 12–18in (30–45cm) depending on variety and situation. It branches freely very close to soil level, producing slender stems and light green leaves about 2in (5cm) long. White or blue flowers appear near the top of each branch throughout the season.

Leaves turn bronze, plant windswept with twisted foliage. Strong winds. Protect by moving container or screening with stronger plants.

Puckered growing points, small insects round unopened buds and stem tips. Aphid. Spray with derris following maker's instructions.

Plant and flowers wilt suddenly. Soil too dry. Water immediately, then keep always moist. Spray.

Plant turns black and soggy. Frost damage. No cure. Protect from frost at all times.

Hanging baskets

1. Line wire basket with moss. Make 5 or 6 small holes in sheet of polythene and lay over moss. Add saucer of charcoal.

2. Stand basket on bucket and fill with layer of damp compost.

3. Knock plant from pot and place in centre of basket, arranging trailing stems evenly all round.

4. Fill with compost and firm round roots. Water well, allow to drain, then hang securely.

Stem turns light brown, especially end of shoots, sometimes with fluffy grey mould. Botrytis. Spray with benomyl, repeat after 10 days, then 1 month later. Botrytis attacks when humidity high, starting on decaying flowers or damaged leaves/stems. Remove all dead flowers and leaves.

Blue flowers pale, petals have brown edges. Too strong sunlight. Protect from sun when over 70°F (21°C).

Tiny white flies, especially on underside of leaves, often with scaly deposits. Whitefly. Spray with diluted malathion every 3 days until clear. Scales will hatch daily so kill each new batch of flies as they appear until all scale gone.

Shoots become thinner, paler and lean towards light. Too dark. Move into lighter place; check plant not heavily screened by others.

what goes wrong

Leaves near base of stems turn pale yellow. Plant often dry or needs more feeding. Do not allow to dry out. If kept moist, increase feed to weekly; do not increase strength of feed.

Plant ceases to develop. Examine compost round roots for tiny, almost transparent grubs, larvae of sciarid or mushroom fly. Drench compost with diluted malathion. Grubs will come to surface and die.

Buds drop off or turn yellow, few flowers open. Waterlogged. Clear drainage holes and allow compost to become nearly dry before watering again.

23

Calendula officinalis

Pot marigold

Pot marigolds are hardy annuals which need full sun and grow quickly. The flowers have a strong scent and last well for more than a week when cut. Double at first, they become smaller and single as the season progresses. Seeds can be sown successively through the early summer, making this a useful plant for filling in any gaps caused by losses in other varieties. They self-sow very easily and may become a nuisance for this reason. To prevent unwanted plants, remove dead flower heads before the seeds form.

Light: Maximum possible.
Temperature: Germinate outdoors at 45°F (7°C), indoors 50°F (10°C). If higher, need very good light. Will stand frost.
Water: Moist, not wet. Will survive quite dry conditions once germinated.
Humidity: Keep dry. Do not spray or water mature plants overhead.
Soil: Will survive poor soil; loam-based No. 1 good.
Feeding: Begin 3 weeks after planting, then every 10 days diluting as maker recommends.
Propagation: Sow outdoors direct into prepared container from mid-spring to early summer. Place seeds ⅜ (9mm) below surface, 4in (10cm) apart and thin to 12in (30cm) apart. For early flowers, sow indoors in prepared seed tray, at 50°F (10°C). Germination takes 3 days. Prick off after 1 week and keep cool (45°F, 7°C) and light. Plant out when 3–4in (7–10cm) high, 4 to a 12in (30cm) container.
Tidying: Remove dead flowers to prevent self-seeding.
Varieties: Radar, deep orange, double with rolled petals (18in, 45cm). Fiesta Gitana, early, good for windowboxes (12in, 30cm). Orange King (12in, 30cm).

Pot marigolds grow to about 18in (45cm) high and have a woody stem with several shoots appearing from near the base. Flower buds come one at a time and may have double or single petals in primrose, yellow or deep orange. The seeds ripen early and will produce new plants the same year.

Swellings on stem and flower stem. Crown gall caused by infected soil splashing on stems. Will not seriously affect flowering. Stand plants hardening off in clean area, not near rubbish.

Leaves have round, dark spots, turning sooty. Smut fungus. Spores will spread. Spray with bordeaux mixture every 14 days.

Leaves and stems covered with white powdery deposit. Powdery mildew. Spray with dinocap or benomyl every 10 days. Plant very susceptible.

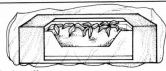

Hardening off

Young plants sown indoors need protecting when first put outside. Place trays close to wall for extra warmth and cover with cardboard box and plastic sheet for first few nights. After 1 week leave uncovered unless weather very bad. Frost will not harm them. Plant in final container after about 10 days.

Removing flowers

Remove seed head as soon as flowers die. Cut off cleanly at top of stalk. If left on, seeds will sow themselves around plant, flowering the same year.

Flower stems long and droopy, flower buds may not open. Too dark. Move into very good light – needs full sun.

Tips of leaves turn black. Overfeeding or too concentrated feed. Never exceed recommended strength.

Plant yellow and sickly, soil surface scummy. Waterlogged. Check drainage in container. Plant prefers dry soil to wet.

Leaves chewed, flower buds have holes. Caterpillar damage. Pick off pests and dust with derris. If petals have holes and ragged edges, earwigs. Dust with gamma-BHC.

Leaves droop and lie limply along stems. Too dry. Will stand all but completely dried out soil. Give container thorough soak so soil is wet right to bottom; then drain to moist before watering again.

what goes wrong

Leaves grey green, stems very woody, flowers small. Needs feeding. Feed every 10 days.

Pinpoint holes in leaves of young plants. Flea beetle. Dust very lightly with gamma-BHC. Avoid edible plants.

Dwarf conifers

Trees in this family vary in height from 24in (60cm) after 10 years growth to 200ft (60m), so it is important to choose the right form for your container. Windowboxes need very dwarf trees. However, a very young dwarf tree will take many years to make a good display and a larger one is costly. Buy a medium-growing species and move it when it gets too big. There is a wide choice suitable for patios and balconies. Conifers should not be pruned. Best time to plant is early to mid-autumn and early to mid-spring. Young trees can be obtained either pot grown or dug from a nursery. Choose healthy, vigorous plants with no brown foliage. Always plant new trees at the same depth as at the nursery, using soil line around trunk as a guide. Deeper planting encourages root disease.

These decorative trees have layers of branches growing out almost horizontally from the stem and small, compressed leaves in various shades of green, some almost blue, others yellow. Small round cones bear the seeds. Make sure you buy the right sized plant for your container.

Light: Good, but shade tolerated.
Temperature: They stand most weathers but may get brown patches from frost.
Water: Do not leave dry or plant in dry area. Foliage will turn brown.
Humidity: Spray with hosepipe or watering can in hot dry spells or long windy periods in spring and autumn.
Soil: Loam-based No.2 best.
Feeding: Every 14 days at maker's recommended strength.
Propagation: By cuttings (see right). Seed is difficult to buy and takes a long time.
Tidying: Unnecessary. Do not prune.
Varieties: Windowboxes; Obtusa nana, Minima aurea, Pisefera nana. Patios, balconies: Lawson fletcheri, Elwoods Gold, Pisefera Boulevard, Filefera aurea. These make 3–5ft (1.6m) trees after several years. There are many others.

Cuttings

1. Cuttings can be taken at any time. Choose branch about 4in (10cm) long and cut cleanly. Trim end and dip in hormone rooting powder.

2. Prepare 3in (9cm) pot with seedling compost and insert branch about 1½in (4cm) into compost. Firm compost round base.

3. Water well and place in sealed plastic bag. Remove cover after 3 weeks.

what goes wrong

Tree does not grow well after frost or produce new leaves; leaves look dull. Frosted roots. Protect exposed containers with straw, sacking or newspapers and cover with plastic to keep them dry when very severe frost expected.

Tips of branchlets turn brown. Too dry. Water thoroughly, always make sure soil is soaked to bottom of container. Make sure container has plenty of drainage material in base before planting or heavy watering will wash soil into drainage holes and clog them.

Foliage turns yellow on any part. May be conifer spinning mite, especially if in early summer. Spray every 14 days with diluted malathion for 2 months.

One side of tree turns brown, rest healthy. Very cold winds in winter, hard frost or marked regularly by cats. During hard winters, place tub in sheltered position.

Fungi at foot of tree, fungal threads under bark. Honey fungus. No cure, destroy plant and do not plant another for 2 years. Do not plant these trees if fungus present in garden though in tub of sterile loam plant should be protected.

Tree turns yellow from base. Root rot disease. Overwatering and waterlogging may start problem so always make sure container well drained. If disease is phytophthora, tree unlikely to survive.

27

Convolvulus tricolor

Dwarf morning glory

This plant has little in common with the rampant weed known as *Convolvulus,* though it, too, grows easily and it gives a mass of colour from just a few seeds. It can be sown where it is to flower, germinates easily, will survive frost and is not too troubled by pests and disease. In colder climates it should be started in a cold frame for protection. An ideal plant for filling out containers (for example where an evergreen has yet to reach a good size), one packet of seeds will fill 6 windowboxes with a blue carpet of flowers.

Dwarf morning glory is a bushy, compact plant about 12in (30cm) high with medium green leaves wider at the tip than the base. The bell-shaped flowers, usually deep blue with a strong yellow centre, bloom through most of the summer.

Light: Sun, but will take an hour or two of shade.
Temperature: Germination, 50–55°F (10–13°C). Will stand frost.
Humidity: Dry, but after a very hot day give a light spray.
Soil: Rich but light such as loam-based No.2.
Feeding: Feed when the seedlings are 4–5 weeks old, using a liquid fertilizer at maker's recommended strength. Repeat every 10 days until early autumn.
Propagation: Sow in mid-spring. If sowing in final container, fill with potting compost to 2in (5cm) from top, water and drain for 2 hours. Add 1in (2½cm) seedling compost and level off with flat board. Water again and drain for 3–4 hours. Sow seed (about 20 to a 12in, 30cm) container) and cover with ⅛in (2mm) compost. A few strands of black cotton will deter birds. Thin seedlings to 10. Or, sow in small pots, 3 to a pot, and place in cold frame. Transfer to final container when about 3in (7cm) high.
Tidying: Remove any yellow leaves.
Varieties: Blue Flash, deep rich blue with yellow centre and white surround. Petite Mixed, rose, blue and white shades with white centre.

White froth, especially where leaf joins stem. Froghopper, concealed in froth. Wash off with hose or spray with diluted malathion at half maker's recommended strength.

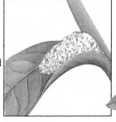

what goes wrong

Plant loose in soil, may be rocking about. Earthworms entering through drainage holes disturbing compost round roots. Worm casts on soil surface confirm. Water with solution of permanganate of potash to bring worms to surface; then remove by hand. Raise container on bricks to prevent further access.

Whole plant droops. Too dry. Give container thorough soak, then allow to become just moist before watering again.

Whole plant yellow and sickly. Waterlogged. Check drainage holes not clogged and water less. Allow to drain until almost dry before watering again.

Spraying

When temperature over 80°F (27°C) mist spray or syringe plants all over in the evening. Do not spray in bright sunlight.

Protecting

Place sticks around edge of container and stretch black cotton between them to deter birds.

Clusters of tiny insects smother growing points. Aphids. Spray with primicarb or other insecticide. Repeat in 10 days if not quite clear.

Leaves have white wriggly lines. Leaf miner. Spray with diluted malathion and repeat after 10 days to kill larvae. Or press finger nail into leaf at end of trail, where grub shows as darker area.

Plant loses colour and does not thrive. Needs feeding. Feed every week instead of every 10 days but do not increase strength of feed.

Some stems wilt while rest of plant fresh. If base of stem damaged, slugs. Slime trails will confirm. If eaten cleanly through, woodlice. Put down slug bait as maker recommends or spray with gamma-BHC for woodlice. Keep both cures away from fishponds; gamma-BHC will taint edible crops grown in same soil following years. Kill woodlice by hand if possible instead.

29

Ornamental gourd

The ornamental gourd is so called because its ripe fruits, lacquered to make them waterproof, last up to a year as indoor decorations. As a patio or balcony plant it will rapidly cover a trellis or trail over a balcony, growing about 10ft (3m) in a season. Originating in the tropics, it likes high humidity and should be protected from wind. Undoubtedly a plant for those who like a challenge.

Light: Good but not full sun for young plants. Mature plants take full sun or dappled sunlight, not shade.
Temperature: Germination 70°F (21°C). Likes high temperatures and humidity and will not grow well under 50°F (10°C).
Water: Never dry, never waterlogged. Needs perfect drainage so that it can be given copious water when hot.
Humidity: As high as possible. Mist spray 2 or 3 times a day in hot weather.
Soil: Mix 50% lumpy sterilized loam with 30% coarse peat or strawy manure and 20% gritty sand. Soil-less potting compost may be used but sinks with regular watering and must be topped up.
Feeding: Feed seedlings at every 5th watering, increasing to every other watering when 2–3ft (30–60cm). Dilute to half maker's recommended strength.
Propagation: Indoors in late spring. Sow seeds singly, on end, in soil-less damp seedling compost in a 3½in (9cm) pot. Keep at 70°F (21°C) and water a little each day. When seedlings appear, move into light and increase watering. Keep warm, cooling gradually to outside temperature for planting out in early summer after all frost has gone.
Tidying: Remove yellow or broken leaves.
Varieties: Seed sold as a mixture.

These climbing annuals are related to the cucumber and have large leaves 9in (23cm) across which tend to hide the flowers and fruit. The flowers are bell-shaped and a deep buttercup yellow. Fruits vary and can be round, long, oval or pear shaped in a variety of colours and patterns.

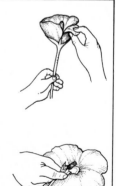

Mottling on foliage. If green, mild virus infection; no cure but growth little affected. If yellow-brown, fruits will also be marked and distorted. Remove plant with care if other gourds in same container – but if aphids on plants earlier, all will eventually show same symptoms.

Pollination

1. If flowers are not pollinated, fruit will not develop. Usually bees and other insects do this for you but if they are rare, pollinate by hand. Remove male flower (with no sign of small fruit below petals) and strip back petals to reveal pollen head.

2. Insert pollen head into centre of female flower (with embryo fruit beginning to show below flower) and gently dust pollen from one flower to the other.

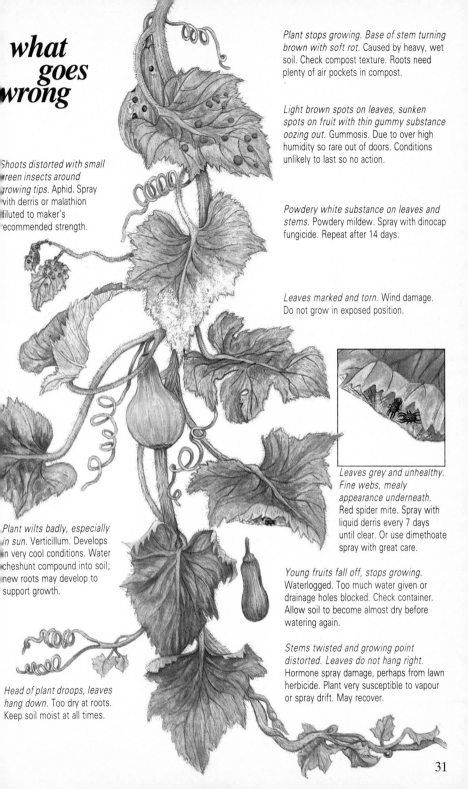

what goes wrong

Plant stops growing. Base of stem turning brown with soft rot. Caused by heavy, wet soil. Check compost texture. Roots need plenty of air pockets in compost.

Light brown spots on leaves, sunken spots on fruit with thin gummy substance oozing out. Gummosis. Due to over high humidity so rare out of doors. Conditions unlikely to last so no action.

Shoots distorted with small green insects around growing tips. Aphid. Spray with derris or malathion diluted to maker's recommended strength.

Powdery white substance on leaves and stems. Powdery mildew. Spray with dinocap fungicide. Repeat after 14 days.

Leaves marked and torn. Wind damage. Do not grow in exposed position.

Leaves grey and unhealthy. Fine webs, mealy appearance underneath. Red spider mite. Spray with liquid derris every 7 days until clear. Or use dimethoate spray with great care.

Plant wilts badly, especially in sun. Verticillum. Develops in very cool conditions. Water cheshunt compound into soil; new roots may develop to support growth.

Young fruits fall off, stops growing. Waterlogged. Too much water given or drainage holes blocked. Check container. Allow soil to become almost dry before watering again.

Stems twisted and growing point distorted. Leaves do not hang right. Hormone spray damage, perhaps from lawn herbicide. Plant very susceptible to vapour or spray drift. May recover.

Head of plant droops, leaves hang down. Too dry at roots. Keep soil moist at all times.

Dahlia

Dahlias vary in height and for most containers bedding or dwarf plants are best. Natives of Mexico, they are very tender and young plants must be carefully protected from spring frosts. At the end of the season when frost has killed the leaves, dig up the tubers, dry thoroughly and dust with fungicide. Store in dry sand, peat or old newspapers in a frost-free place until late winter.

Light: Good at all times.
Temperature: Germination and cuttings, 60°–65°F (16–18°C). Outside, little growth below 45°F (7°C).
Water: keep moist but not soggy.
Humidity: Spray seedlings and cuttings, not mature plants.
Soil: Loam-based No. 3 or soil-less.
Feeding: Start 14 days after planting, at recommended strength, then every 10 days for loam-based, every 5 for soil-less composts.
Propagation: Prepare seed tray in early spring. Sow and cover with ¼in (7mm) compost; put in plastic bag at 60–65°F (16–18°C) until seedlings appear. Move to full light. Prick out when large enough to handle but do not plant out until frosts finished. From tubers, plant in trays of soil or soil-less compost in late winter, covering tuber but not crown. Water a little each day. When shoots 3in (8cm) long, cut them off right down to tuber and dip ends in rooting powder. Plant 1in (2½cm) deep in seedling compost in 3in (9cm) pots. They root in 3 weeks. Then treat as seedlings.
Tidying: Remove dead flowers. Take off buds below main flower to improve its size.
Varieties: From seed Coltness Gem, red or yellow, single dwarf, double or semi-double. Figaro, dwarf, early, many colours. Redskin, dwarf, bushy, mixed colours.

Dahlia flowers come in almost every colour and shade from red through yellow to white, in single, semi-double and double blooms. To be sure of getting the shape and colour of flower you want, buy cuttings from a dahlia specialist; but plants can also be successfully grown from seed.

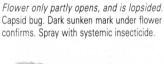

Flower only partly opens, and is lopsided. Capsid bug. Dark sunken mark under flower confirms. Spray with systemic insecticide.

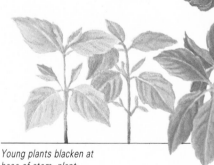

Young plants blacken at base of stem, plant yellowing. Root or stem rot. Treat with soil fungicide but do not plant out affected plants.

Plant grows straggly and weak. Not enough light. Dahlias need good light at all times.

Young plant turns yellow, soil dark and sour. Waterlogged. Check drainage in container.

Grey mould on flowers. Botrytis. Spray with benomyl. Do not spray mature plants with water.

Young plants yellow, leaves pale but compost not too wet. Needs feeding. Feed every 10 days in loam-based soil, every 5 in soil-less compost. If feeding intervals correct, feed more often but do not use stronger food.

Seedlings or young plants outside turn black overnight. Frost. Protect from frost in spring.

Young growth has small spots gradually enlarging. Sooty moulds develop. Smut disease. Spray weekly with bordeaux mixture.

Plant has holes and looks chewed. If flowers ragged with small holes in petals, earwigs. Trap in upturned pot or jar filled with dry grass or straw and destroy. Or, use gamma-BHC with care. If leaves, flowers and buds eaten with many holes and slimy trails, slugs or snails. Put down slug pellets as maker instructs. Keep away from animals and fish ponds.

Holes in leaves, flower buds eaten. Caterpillar. Search for pest and remove. Or use gamma-BHC with care.

Shoots, buds and flowers have clusters of small insects. Aphid. Spray with malathion or systemic insecticide. Repeat weekly until clear.

Streaky silver marks on leaves, possibly flowers distorted. Thrips. Small flies may be flying round plant. Spray with malathion or other insecticide.

Irregular blackish streaks, some yellow mottling on leaves. Virus disease. Will not badly affect flowers but do not use for cuttings. If aphids around, do not use any plants for cuttings as disease will spread.

what goes wrong

Flower droops. Too dry. Water immediately and keep soil always moist but not waterlogged.

Dianthus

As Dianthus species cross easily there are many hybrids. All are suitable for containers as are the many annual and perennial species. Recent hybrids, all annuals, have the longest flowering periods, from early to late summer. If buying plants in spring, choose bushy, healthy ones as they will produce more flowers.

Light: Maximum at all times.
Temperature: Winter germination 60°F (16°C). After pricking out, 50°F (10°C).
Water: For germination, moist. Otherwise almost dry, well-drained soil.
Humidity: Dry. Do not spray.
Soil: Well-drained, sandy, or loam-based No.2. Plants grown for 1 season only may be in soil-less compost.
Feeding: Liquid fertilizer every 14 days in soil, every 7 in soil-less. Perennials in second and later years benefit from soil dressing of nitrochalk (5g per plant) but this must not touch plant.
Germination: Sow annuals as soon as days start to lengthen, on surface of well-drained seedling compost. Cover with ⅛in (2mm) dry compost and brown paper. Germination takes about 10 days. Prick out as soon as large enough to handle. Sow perennials in early summer in cold frame in shade. Plant out in early autumn for summer flowering. Perennials can be layered or propagated from cuttings.
Tidying: Pick off seed pods.
Varieties: Annuals: Magic Charms, bushy, strong, mixed colours (6in, 15cm). Snow-fire, white with cherry eye (12in, 30cm). Queen of Hearts, brilliant scarlet (12in, 30cm). Telstar, long flowering, mixed colours (9in, 20cm). Perennials: Spring Beauty, early flowering, mixed colours (12in, 30cm). Deltoides Flashing Lights, ruby red, (12in, 30cm). Alpinus, very small and compact.

Dianthus has a woody base from which grow light green branching stems, each ending with a single flower. Flower colours range from white through to pink and red and blooms may be bicoloured. There is also a pale yellow variety. Most have very narrow leaves, a few are even grass-like.

Plant turns yellow from base. If stem blackening, waterlogged. Check drainage holes and allow to dry out between waterings. Use less water. If top growth also wilts in hot weather, recovering by early morning, carnation wilt disease. Cut stem and if core discoloured, remove plant and destroy. Sterilize soil with fungicide. If only 1 shoot affected, cut off and burn. Plant may survive. Do not use affected plants for cuttings.

what goes wrong

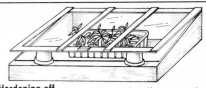

Small dark spots on leaves, erupting to form reddish powdery deposits. Rust disease. Spray with copper based fungicide to maker's instructions.

Plant grows leggy not bushy. Too hot while growing indoors. Keep at 50°F (10°C) while at seedling stage.

Hardening off
For good flower production keep young plants cool. When seedlings growing, cool gradually to temperature of outside cold frame and transplant. Keep covered with glass for 1 week, then raise glass during day except in snow or heavy frost. Move to final container in early to mid-spring.

Black sooty deposit in centre of open flowers. Leaves or buds distorted. Anther smut. Remove and destroy plant to prevent spread. Not common on annuals.

Small clusters of lice on new growth or flowers. Aphid. Spray in the evening with pirimicarb.

Young plant just taken outside turns very dark. Frost or cold wind. Protect during first week outside and at night. Will probably recover but not grow well.

Plant droops and wilts. Much too dry. Water immediately but make sure container is well drained as plant prefers dry conditions.

Spots with reddish edges on leaves. Dianthus ring spot. Spray every 10 days with bordeaux mixture until clear.

Leaves pale, plant does not grow but no obvious pests or diseases. Examine base of plant for root aphid. If found, spray with diluted malathion to maker's instructions. If no aphid, needs feeding. Feed every 14 days in soil, every 7 in soil-less compost. If feeding regularly feed more often.

Seedlings have very thin stem near soil and later fall over. Pythium disease. Unlikely in sterile soil and cool temperatures. Prick out unaffected seedlings. Do not use diseased ones or those around them. Treat soil with fungicide.

Cape marigold

These graceful, lightweight flowers are attractive in both tubs and window-boxes. They are generally grown as annuals and need a warm sheltered spot since they are half hardy. Seed can be sown directly in the container or, more easily, indoors in gentle heat. They can also be sown in peat pots and transferred intact to the container.

Light: The best at all times.
Temperature: Germination, 60–65°F (16–18°C). Young seedlings, 50–55°F (10–13°C). Outside, a warm sheltered sunny spot. No frost.
Water: Keep moist. Water little and often.
Humidity: Dry, no spraying overhead.
Soil: Either loam–based No.2 or soil-less potting compost. Do not press compost down too firmly or water cannot drain away.
Feeding: Liquid fertilizer at maker's recommended strength every 14 days in soil, every 7 days in soil-less.
Propagation: Sow seed thinly on surface of prepared, drained seedling compost in early spring. Sprinkle fine dry compost to just cover seeds. Place in 60–65°F (16–18°C) under paper cover. Seedlings will transplant more easily if pricked out as soon as large enough to handle. Place in full light. Or sow in peat pots, thinning out to 2–3 seedlings per pot. Then transfer to container in pots. If using mixed hybrid seed, do not choose only the largest seedlings when thinning. They may be all the same colour.
Tidying: Remove dead flowers, cutting stems right down for neatness.
Varieties: Aurantiaca hybrids, orange, salmon, pale yellow, apricot and white; very graceful (12in, 30cm). Aurantiaca Dwarf Salmon, ideal for windowboxes. Aurantiaca Giant Orange (12in, 30cm). Glistening White and Las Vegas (mixed) both 18in (45cm).

The Cape marigold's flowers, up to 4in (10cm) across, grow singly on a rather thin stem and usually close towards late afternoon, opening again the following morning. Colours range from apricot through salmon pink to pale yellow and white.

Silvery streaks on leaves, flowers may be distorted. Thrips. Spray with systemic insecticide to maker's instructions. Do not spray during day.

Small dark spots on leaves. Leaf spot fungus. Spray with bordeaux mixture or ipridione.

Foliage sticky, possibly with sooty deposit. Small insects oin buds. Aphid. Spray with pirimicarb.

Young plants in trays or peat pots eaten off at soil level. Woodlice. Trace hiding place and destroy. Use gamma-BHC with care. Common where there is undisturbed litter.

Flowers tattered, buds ragged. Earwig damage. Pests hide during day under debris, inside canes or crevices. Trap in small plant pot filled with dry grass or straw, balanced upside down on short stick. Empty trapped pests into boiling water each morning. Dust areas carefully with gamma-BHC.

Sowing in peat pots
1. Water pots and allow to drain gor 2–3 hours. Sprinkle seed thinly on surface.

2. Cover with sprinkling of fine dry compost and place under paper cover in 60–65°F (16–18°C).

3. When seedlings large enough to handle, thin out weaker ones, leaving 2–3 per pot. Plant whole pot in container.

what goes wrong

Few flowers appear or flower buds do not open. Too dark. Plant must be in good bright light.

Flowers small, leaves lose freshness. Too dry. If moisture correct, needs feeding. Increase number but not strength of feeds.

Brown scorch marks on leaf and petal tips. Fertilizer too strong or sprayed in sunshine or cold winds. Check conditions. Do not use fertilizer stronger than maker recommends or spray in sun. Protect against strong cold winds.

Large holes in leaves near ground. Slugs or snails. Place slug pellets round plant as maker recommends. Remove dying slugs which may recover in warm, moist weather.

Plant does not thrive, some leaves turn yellow. Too wet. Allow container to dry out before watering again and check drainage holes clear. If watering correct, scarape away some soil from roots to see if root aphids present. If so, water with diluted malathion.

White froth on leaves. Froghopper sucking sap under froth. Pinch between finger and thumb to remove or if very many present, spray with diluted malathion.

Plant collapses and leaves turn black. Frost damage. Will not survive frosts. Protect in spring.

Eccremocarpus scaber

Chilean glory flower

This half-hardy perennial climber (a native of Chile) will survive winters in warmer climates but is usually treated as an annual where winters are cold. It grows best on a sunny patio or balcony wall, well sheltered from the wind, in any type of fertile soil. It has a slightly ribbed, almost square stem with long sappy tendrils by which it climbs. If there is nothing for the tendrils to cling to, it also does well as a trailing plant.

Light: Maximum, though 2–3 hours shade tolerated. Must be very good when indoors in early spring.
Temperature: Germination, 70°F (21°C), reducing gradually to 45°F (7°C) before planting out. Will stand temperatures down to 40°F (5°C) if there is no wind.
Water: Moist. Water in early morning. If in 8in (20cm) pot, check soil regularly as it will dry out quickly.
Humidity: Do not spray.
Soil: Loam-based No. 2 or soil-less potting compost. Or homemade mix if sterile and well drained.
Feeding: Every 10 days for loam-based, every 5 for soil-less. Start when it has been in its final container for 1 week. Use liquid, dry or stick fertilizer, following maker's instructions.
Propagation: Sow in early spring on prepared seedling compost. Dust over with dry compost and leave at 70°F (21°C). Seedlings appear quickly and together. Give good light. When large enough to handle, prick out into small pots, plastic packs or peat pots so that roots are not disturbed later. Harden off gradually, planting outside when risk of frost has passed. An 8in (20cm) pot is adequate for 1 plant for 1 season.
Tidying: Remove any wind-damaged stems.
Varieties: No other varieties.

Chilean glory flowers can grow to 8ft (over 2½m) in a season producing their clusters of deep orange, scarlet or yellow flowers in midsummer. Each flower is tubular, just over 1in (2½cm) long, flaring open at the end. The deep green oval leaves are slightly serrated.

Training a climbing plant

Fasten plastic net to wall and position pot in centre. Attach stem to net with plant rings or ties or loop thin string around them as shown. Do not tie knot against stem as it may damage the tissues. Spread branching stems in the direction you wish plant to grow.

Young plants outside before planting suddenly collapse. Stem separated from root at soil level. Woodlice damage. Search for pest under tray or container and kill. Dust area carefully with gamma-BHC.

what goes wrong

Head of plant hangs down, leaves droopy. Too dry. Water more often and more copiously to keep soil moist.

White froth where leaf joins stem. Froghopper. Kill by squeezing between finger and thumb or wash off with jet of water. Spray with systemic insecticide to prevent return.

White lines on leaves. Leaf miner. Insect is inside plant tissue. Press fingernail into leaf at end of trail to destroy or if attack severe, spray with systemic insecticide.

Stems weak and pale with few flowers. Too much shade. Plant needs sun for most of the day.

Leaves pale and small. Needs feeding. If compost home-made mix, was fertilizer incorporated? If not, topdress with enriched compost or feed more frequently. Do not increase strength of fertilizer.

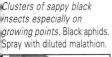

Clusters of sappy black insects especially on growing points. Black aphids. Spray with diluted malathion.

Growing point and flower buds distorted with small insects clustered. Aphid. Spray with liquid derris or diluted malathion. Repeat in 10 days if not clear.

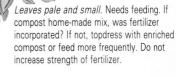

Edges of leaves near base chewed. Slugs or snails. Stems may also be damaged. Place slug pellets around area following maker's instructions. Keep away from pets and fish ponds.

Plant does not thrive, soil surface dark and scummy. Overwatered; drainage holes may be blocked. Clear holes and allow soil to dry out before watering again.

Strawberry

Strawberries can be successfully grown in windowboxes, tubs or in special strawberry barrels if they are in an open position in good light. The fruits should be raised off the soil and special mats which fit around the plant like a collar are available. For a good crop the following year, plant in midsummer; if planting later, pick off the first flowers next year to build up a vigorous plant for autumn fruiting.

Light: Good, in an open position.

Temperature: Warm, sunny when fruiting. Will survive frost but fruits will not form. Protect from spring frosts.

Water: Never allow to dry out.

Humidity: They need a dry atmosphere. Do not spray when fruiting.

Soil: Loam-based No. 3 or soil-less potting compost or equal parts of each.

Feeding: If planting in midsummer, feed in early autumn with topdressing of bone meal (1oz per sq yd, 28g per sq m). When new growth appears in spring, give liquid feed every week until fruits ripe. For 2nd and 3rd year plants, add fish, blood and bone fertilizer to topsoil in midsummer and feed as first year plants in autumn.

Propagation: Plant produces runners (small plantlets on tips of trailing stems). Peg them to soil with 3in (8cm) wire staples. New plantlets will root by midsummer and can be cut off and transplanted or left in position. Then treat as new plants. Alpine and seed varieties should be sown as soon as days lengthen.

Tidying: Remove yellow leaves. Cut runners off if not propagating or leave as decoration over side of container.

Varieties: Large fruiting and heavy cropping are Cambridge Favourite, Pantagruella, Red Gauntlet. Seed variety, Sweetheart. Alpine variety, Baron Solemacher.

The strawberry's white flowers are followed by delicious red fruits which vary in flavour and size according to variety. New plants can be propagated from the trailing runners but since they are prone to virus diseases, buy certified disease free plants to be sure of a healthy crop.

Small colonies of insects on leaves and growing points. Aphid. Many kinds feed on strawberries and spread virus diseases. Spray with diluted malathion every 10 days until flowers open. Do not spray when in flower or bees will be killed.

what goes wrong

Grey mould on leaves and fruit, especially if fruit is damaged. Botrytis. Spray in late evening with benomyl.

Leaves drab with pink scurfy look underneath. Red spider mite. Spray with derris from early spring until flowers open to prevent attack. If not in flower, spray with diluted malathion.

Leaves crinkled with brown marks on upper side; feel hard and brittle. Tarsonemid mite. Spray in late evening with liquid derris. Check maker's instructions before picking sprayed fruit.

Flowers turn brown overnight. Frost. Fruit will not set on affected flowers. Protect flowering plants from frost.

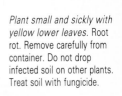

Plant small and sickly with yellow lower leaves. Root rot. Remove carefully from container. Do not drop infected soil on other plants. Treat soil with fungicide.

Plant does not grow well, soil surface dark and scummy. Overwatered. Check drainage in container and allow excess to drain away before watering again. But do not allow to dry out completely.

Holes in ripening fruit. Birds or, if also slimy trails, slugs. Destroy any visible slugs and put down slug pellets following maker's instructions. Keep away from pets and fishponds. Protect from birds with cotton or netting.

Small red, grey or purple spots on leaves. Leaf spot disease. Spray with bordeaux mixture.

Flower buds eaten off, lying on soil or hanging limply. Possibly blossom weevil. Pick off and burn affected buds. Spraying with diluted malathion before flowers open will prevent attack.

Leaves dry and brown, fruits small. Too dry. Keep soil moist, never allowing container to dry out.

White powder on stems and fruit. Powdery mildew. Dust in late spring with sulphur dust to prevent attacks.

Lacy holes in leaves, flowers eaten and fruit marked. Moth caterpillar, possibly between leaves that are folded over with fine threads. Pick off affected leaves and dust plant with derris dust.

41

Treasure flower

Of South African origin, the Treasure flower is a sun worshipper and is ideally suited to a windowbox where heavy rain rarely soaks the soil as it would in a garden. The large flowers close during late afternoon, though never completely. Usually grown as an annual, they can be kept from year to year if winter temperatures are moderate but are best taken into a greenhouse or conservatory at the end of summer. Buy plants that are not too crowded in the tray, with good green colouring. Unless plants in pots or small containers, buds should not be visible.

Light: Best at all times.

Temperature: Germination 65°F (18°C), cooling gradually to outside conditions. Outside, will stand very high temperatures but not frost.

Water: Except while a seedling, prefers dry conditions. Soak container thoroughly, then leave until almost dry before watering again.

Humidity: No overhead spraying.

Soil: Loam-based No. 2 or soil-less potting compost.

Feeding: Feed every 14 days in loam-based, every 7 in soil-less, at maker's recommended strength.

Propagation: Sow seed as soon as days start to lengthen, on surface of well-drained seedling compost. Cover with ⅛in (2mm) dry compost and brown paper. Germination takes about 10 days. Prick out as soon as large enough to handle. Or, take cuttings in early midsummer.

Tidying: Cut off dead flowers at base of stem. Do not damage crown of plant.

Varieties: Mini Star, clear yellow (8in, 20cm), a European medal winner. Sunshine hybrids, large flowered mixed with stripes and dark zones (12in, 30cm). Splendens mixed (12in, 30cm).

A single Gazania flower may be as large as 4in (10cm) in diameter. Petals are usually pointed and many have a dark, round spot at the base which forms a necklace around the central zone. The leaves, crowded at the plant's base, grow to 6–9in (15–20cm) in height.

Leaves thin and pale. Much too dry. Soak soil then allow to dry out. If watering regular, needs feeding. Feed regularly for bright leaves and flowers.

Cuttings

1. Cut side shoot from outside of clump with sharp knife. Shoot should be about 4in (10cm) long. Trim off lowest leaf and dip end in rooting powder.

2. Place in 3in (9cm) pot of seedling compost. Water well and place in frame or protect from wind with glass. In full sun, protect with hessian. Rooting takes 4–6 weeks. Take indoors by mid-autumn and keep dry, cool and airy. Repot into larger pot in early spring.

what goes wrong

Leaves turn yellow, flowers distorted. Virus. No cure. Destroy plant and do not use same soil for other plantings.

Plant does not thrive, leaves turn yellow gradually and few flowers appear. Root rot, possibly from overwatering. Allow soil to dry out and plant may recover. It prefers dry conditions.

White froth on leaves. Froghopper. Pick off by hand or remove with jet of water. If badly affected, spray with diluted malathion.

Clusters of small insects, especially on buds. Aphid. Spray with pirimicarb and repeat after 10 days if not clear.

White dots or flecks on leaf surface. Underside mealy and pinkish. Red spider mite. Spray with dimethoate and repeat in 14 days.

Silvery white markings on leaves. Thrips. Spray with diluted malathion.

Soil surface erupts with fine dry mound of soil. Ants nesting or cultivating aphids on plant. Dust surface of soil with derris dust. Will not attack plant but will loosen its hold on soil.

Some leaves become limp. Probably slug attacking roots. Place slug pellets around plant, following maker's instructions but keep away from pets and fishponds. Remove dead pest.

Veronica

Hebes make attractive, long-lasting shrubs which can tolerate high winds if not subjected to heavy frosts. There are hardy dwarf varieties for windowboxes and a wide range of taller ones for patios and balconies. They may need protection from winter weather depending on where you live. Build a shelter round them or move them to a sheltered spot. Summer quarters should be sunny.

Light: Plenty, though they can take about 3 hours shade. Indoors, best light possible.
Temperature: Most survive mild frosts and, if well watered, stand high temperatures.
Water: Keep moist but well drained in summer. In winter water only enough to stop soil drying out completely.
Humidity: Spray overhead when 70°F (21°C).
Soil: Loam-based No. 2.
Feeding: Regular summer feeding with liquid or dry organic fertilizers, according to maker's instructions.
Propagation: Take cuttings about 4in (10cm) long, at any time between early and late summer. Trim to a point below a leaf joint and remove bottom leaves. Dip into rooting powder and insert in 3½in (9cm) pot, 4 round each pot. Rooting takes about 6 weeks. Then pot each cutting separately.
Tidying: After flowering, cut off flowering stems.
Varieties: For windowboxes: Carl Teschner, violet/blue, in early summer (9in, 22cm). Carnosula, white in mid-summer (6in, 15cm). Pagei, blue grey foliage, white flowers in late spring (9in, 22cm). For patios: Midsummer Beauty, lavender in early-late summer (3ft, 1m). Autumn Glory, purple in early summer – early autumn (2ft, 60cm). Speciosa hybrids, shiny leaves, purple crimson, lavender/rose flowers.

These evergreen flowering shrubs come mainly from New Zealand and vary in height from 6in to 6ft (15cm to 2m). Th flowering season is equally varied, being from late spring to early autumn, in colours ranging from white to blue, purple and even crimson.

Leaves pale grey/green, flowers dull. Too dry. Water thoroughly so that bottom of container is well wetted. Then allow to dry out until surface feels just moist before watering again. If watering correct, needs feeding. Give topdressing of potash organic fertilizer and feed regularly.

Round brown spots with purple outer ring on leaves, some shoots or stems light brown and dying. Hebe leaf spot. Cut out any dying stems and spray with benomyl every 14 days until clear.

Edges of leaves turn brown. Root scorch from too strong fertilizers. Always use maker's recommended strength. Dry fertilizers must be applied only to well watered soil, then well watered in.

Foliage darkens, then turns pale, leaves fall. Frost damage. May recover in spring. Prune off damaged growth in early spring. Protect in winter or move to sheltered position.

44

what goes wrong

tem soft and brown with
ome whitish strands;
vhole shrub turning yellow.
oney fungus. No cure. Burn
lant and do not plant trees
r shrubs in garden for 2
ears. Should not affect
hrubs in containers unless in
ontaminated soil. Watch for
oadstools round base of
ead tree stumps.

Leaves pale and thin, stem growing lanky. Too dark. Move to lighter place.

Pruning

To keep plants compact, prune when flowers have died. For small-leaved plants, trim all round bush with shears.

For large-leaved plants, trim with pruning shears, making cuts just above a leaf. Do not cut through leaves.

Yellowish specks, sometimes pale blisters on leaf surface, whitish mould under. Downy mildew. Spray with bordeaux mixture every 14 days until clear.

Pinpoint white spots on upper surface of leaf, scurfy grey below, with fine webs. Red spider mite. Spray with dimethoate and repeat until new growth clean, at maker's recommended strength and intervals.

Leaves yellow from base of plant, no growth. Waterlogged or root rot, from serious overwatering. Allow soil to drain, check drainage holes and water less often in future.

45

Ivy

The Ivy is a native of northern Europe and so almost completely hardy. It grows in all conditions, from deep shade to full sun, though its leaf colour is best between these extremes. Almost pest and disease free and tolerant of all kinds of weather, it is an ideal plant for container growing. Smaller-leaved dwarf varieties are best for window-boxes and last for many years while there are many vigorous ones to cover large areas. Pruning may be needed to control their growth.

Light: Variegated forms need good light.
Temperature: Survives frost. Cuttings will take quicker at 60°F (16°C), but will take anyway.
Water: Keep moist but not waterlogged.
Humidity: In hot, dry weather (over 70°F, 21°C) give an overhead spray.
Soil: Almost any except solid clay. Loam-based No. 2 is ideal.
Feeding: Liquid or dry fertilizer at maker's recommended strengths and intervals. If using dry fertilizer, water soil first and allow to drain before feeding.
Propagation: In spring or summer, cut off a shoot with aerial roots (most of them have), about 4in (10cm) long. Plant it outdoors or indoors and it will root rapidly. No rooting powder is necessary. Cuttings without aerial roots will also take easily, but after a longer period.
Varieties: Buttercup, small leaved, golden. Glacier, small pale green and white. Chicago, small, green and purple. Tricolour, small silver for windowboxes. *Colchia dentata aurea,* large and fast growing, green splashed gold. *Canariensis,* large thick leaves, green and cream. *Sagitaefolia,* tall, lime green.

The Ivy's evergreen trailing or climbing stems carry aerial roots which cling to walls, trellises or the soil surface and enable its attractive leaves to cover a wide area. The leaves vary in size and colour, some being strongly variegated. The flowers are small but the berries are attractive.

Scales on underside of leaves, close to veins. Scale insect. Wipe off with cotton-wool dipped in methylated spirits.

Humidity
Spray leaves regularly, especially when hot and dry. This keeps them fresh and clean and also helps to prevent attacks of red spider mite.

what goes wrong

eaves eaten near top of plant. Caterpillar. Remove visible pests and dust plant carefully with gamma-BHC.

Wingless insects with white covering on underside of leaves. Mealy bug. Wipe off with cotton-wool dipped in methylated spirits and spray with dimethoate.

Small insects on stem tips, leaves sticky and sooty. Aphid. Spray with pirimicarb. Repeat after 10 days.

Edges of leaves brown and dry. Wind damage if plant buffeted about. Plant will grow on but leaves may fall.

White powdery deposit on stems. Powdery mildew. Sometimes occurs if plant left dry for long period. Spray with benomyl every 14 days.

Lower leaves turn yellow, stem and leaves dark; some mould on stem. Soil waterlogged. Check and clear drainage holes. Allow soil to dry out before watering again.

Small black flies running over soil surface. Sciarid fly grubs in soil. Drench soil with diluted malathion.

Pale pin-point spots on leaves, leaves fading. Underside mealy, pinkish colour. May be fine webs round leaves. Red spider mite. Spray every 14 days with diluted malathion or dimethoate until clear. Spray regularly with water to prevent attack.

Variegation of leaves not pronounced. Too dark. Plain green varieties best for dark areas. Move into better light if possible.

Leaves grey/green and thin. Too dry or needs feeding. Check conditions. Keep soil moist but not waterlogged and feed regularly.

Edges of leaves dry out and leaves fall. Much too dry. Water immediately. Do not leave for long periods without water. Spray regularly in hot weather.

Small brown or dark spots on leaves. Leaf spot fungus. Spray with fungicide and repeat after 14 days.

Silvery streaks on leaves. Thrips. Spray with diluted malathion or any systemic insecticide. Do not spray in bright sunlight.

Edges of leaves near soil eaten. If slime on soil, slugs or snails. Put down slug pellets as maker recommends. If no slime, woodlice. Dust area carefully with gamma-BHC.

47

Heliotrope

Heliotropes are natives of Peru and can be grown in a number of ways: as a dwarf bushy plant, as a pyramid 24–30in (60–75cm) tall or as a 4ft (120cm) standard. Dwarf varieties are easy to grow in a windowbox and well worth a place for their scent. They will not stand frost and should be planted out in mild weather when all frost has finished. Overwinter them in a greenhouse or conservatory.

Light: Maximum but will stand some hours of shade. Indoors in winter, maximum possible.
Temperature: Germination, 65–70°F (18–21°C). Spring cuttings need bottom heat and surrounding temperature of 60°F (16°C). No frost.
Water: Keep moist, not waterlogged.
Humidity: Syringe after hot days.
Soil: Loam-based No. 2. Soil-less potting compost is suitable for dwarf plants but will not support standards.
Feeding: Every 10 days in loam, every 5 in soil-less, diluted to maker's recommended strength.
Propagation: From seed in early spring. Treat as Browallia (p. 22), pricking off into 3½in (9cm) pots when second pair of leaves formed. Take cuttings in spring or late summer. Summer cuttings should be rooted in seedling compost around the edge of a 3½in (9cm) pot and overwintered at 45°F (7°C). In early spring, cut off the top 3in (8cm) and root each one in 3½in (9cm) pot.
Tidying: Remove dead heads with sharp knife.
Varieties: For general planting, Marine, very dwarf with a strong scent and very deep purple flowers. For training as a standard, Peruvianum, var. Gigantia, lavender, well scented.

Heliotropes are rather sombre looking plants with dark green leaves often overlaid with purple. The purple or white flowers are tiny but grow in large plate-like clusters in the centre of the plant. Their beauty lies mostly in the superb vanilla scent given off especially in the evening.

Flowers tattered or missing. Earwigs. If plants are staked, these may be hiding in the hollow of the bamboo cane. They can be killed by inserting wire into hollow.

Foliage turns very deep colour, almost black. Very cold wind. Move container to more sheltered position.

Fluffy mould on plant during winter indoors. Botrytis. This may develop on butt of removed side shoot or other damaged area. Spray once a month through winter with iprodione.

Edges of leaves turn brown and shrivelled when plant is indoors. Damage from fumes of gas or other heater. Or, damage from insecticide spray in sunshine.

Pinhead whitish spots on leaves, possibly some holes torn. The effect of a heavy hailstorm on broad, tender leaves. Protect plant in bad weather.

what goes wrong

Whole plant droops, leaves wilt. Too dry or overwatered, root rot. Check compost. If dry, water container thoroughly. If soil wet and heavy, check drainage and allow to dry out before watering again. Then keep moist but not soggy. Severe waterlogging will cause root rot and plant will die.

Small white flies on underside of leaves when plant indoors. Small clear scales present. Whitefly. Spray every 3 days with permethrin until all trace of scales and flies has gone.

Training a standard

1. Remove all side shoots from young plant or cutting in spring. Keep moist and feed regularly. Remove flower buds.

2. As stem grows, tie it every 6in (15cm) to a 48in (130cm) cane. Continue to remove side shoots. In early autumn, repot and keep almost dry in cool, light airy place over winter. Do not feed. Repot and start feeding again in early spring.

Leaves and flowers sticky with small flies. Aphid. Spray with pirimicarb. Especially important to prevent aphid on trained plants.

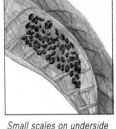

Small scales on underside of leaves, especially while plants growing indoors. Scale insect. Spray with diluted malathion and dab scales with paintbrush dipped in methylated spirits to loosen hold. Then lightly scrape off leaf.

Leaves lose rich colour. Possibly thrips if flecking present. Spray with diluted malathion. If no markings on foliage, plant needs feeding. Feed regularly.

Foliage is black and soggy. Plant has been killed by frost. Heliotrope will not take frost. Protect in late spring when young plants hardening off or just planted.

Holes in leaves. Slugs. Place slug pellets around area as directed by maker. Keep away from pets and fishponds.

Lobelia

Lobelias are half hardy perennials but are invariably grown as annuals from seed sown as soon as the days start to lengthen. Trailing varieties are valuable for containers as they will clothe the side of a tub or trough and hang attractively from a basket or windowbox.

Light: Maximum at all stages. Outside up to 30% shade if light good for rest of the day.
Temperature: 60–65°F (16–18°C) for first month after sowing, reducing gradually to 45°F (7°C) before planting out. Protect from frost.
Water: Moist, not waterlogged.
Humidity: Spray in the evening if hot.
Soil: Well drained loam-based No. 2 or soil-less potting compost.
Feeding: Regular feeding every 10 days in soil or every 5 in soil-less. A liquid fertilizer containing more potash than nitrogen is desirable to keep the intensity of colour and prevent the plant succumbing to disease.
Propagation: Seed is very fine. Prepare tray and mix seed with half its volume of very fine sand. Sow thinly over whole surface of compost. Don't cover seed with compost, but place tray in plastic bag, seal, cover with several layers of newspaper and keep at 60–65°F (16–18°C). Uncover when germinated and prick out when large enough to handle. Plant out when frosts have finished and flowers nearly open.
Tidying: Remove stems which have turned brown from disease.
Varieties: Trailing: Sapphire, dark blue, white eye. Blue Cascade, light blue. Red Cascade, carmine. Compact varieties: Crystal Palace, rich deep blue with bronze foliage. Mrs Clibran, deep blue and white eye. Blue Gown, mid-blue. String of Pearls, mixed.

Lobelias are either dwarf, compact plants only 4–6in (10–15cm) high or trailers with stems up to 24in (60cm) long. The tiny flowers bloom over a very long season and may be white, crimson, violet and from light to very deep blue.

Leaves yellow with dark veining. Soil dark and sour. Waterlogged. Check drainage in container and allow soil to dry out before watering again,

Leaves small and grey-green. Needs feeding. Feed more often but do not increase strength of feed.

Leaves spotted with pale buff-coloured markings, which gradually join up until whole leaf is affected. Stems have streaky marks. Alternaria disease. Spray with iprodione and following week with benomyl. Alternate treatments every fortnight to prevent infection. Contaminated plants will continue to flower but will cease flowering earlier in the season than usual. Alternaria can be seed-borne so make sure purchased seed has been treated against it. But spores can also infect growing plants, especially if wet.

Leaves sag, whole plant flops on soil. Too dry. Water immediately then water more frequently so soil does not dry out.

Young plants turn purple when first put outside. Sudden cold. Plant growth will be checked, but will recover. Introduce plants to outdoors gradually. Protect from frost if out at night.

Seedlings or young plants suddenly wilt and stems are thin, cotton-like strands. Pythium disease or damping off. Remove affected plants and drench compost with soil fungicide.

what goes wrong

Puckered or distorted buds and growing points. Greenfly. Spray with general insecticide and repeat after 10 days. Do not spray in hot sunshine; wait until evening.

Leaves have papery markings on edges. Liquid fertilizer too strong. Always dilute to maker's recommended strength.

Leaves have white, dead edges. Caused by spraying insecticides in sunlight. Spray in the evening, when bees have finished visiting flowers.

Leaves have grey, dry patches. Frost damage. Protect young plants at night and harden off gradually. Lobelias will stand some frost if carefully hardened.

Flowers pale, stems soft. Feed does not contain right balance of potash and nitrogen. More potash than nitrogen is desirable. Check contents of fertilizer.

Fluffy grey mould on leaves or stems or whole crown. Botrytis. Carefully pick off affected areas and spray with benomyl or iprodione. While indoors keep plants in well ventilated position.

Tomato

The Tomato is a native of central America and has been hybridized for a very long time, producing a confusing array of forms, leaf and fruit colours. For containers it is vital to choose a dwarf variety which will not need special training. Planting out time is critical: too early and they will be killed by frost; too late and they will fail to branch and so fruit less prolifically.

Light: Maximum at all times.
Temperature: Germination, 65°F (18°C). Cool to 50°F (10°C) before putting outside. Plant out when all danger of frost is passed.
Water: Seedlings, just moist. Plants need to be always moist. Test compost every day.
Humidity: High. Syringe when indoors. Spray outside in warm sun. Stop spraying by midsummer.
Soil: Peat-based potting compost or loam-based No.2 with ¼ added peat.
Feeding: Feed loam-based soil at every 5th watering, soil-less at every 3rd. Use special tomato fertilizer. Start 14 days after seedlings pricked out, at half maker's recommended strength. Ten days after final planting, increase to recommended dose.
Propagation: Prepare seed tray. Sow and cover with ⅛in (3mm) dry compost. Place in propagator or plastic bag at 65°F (18°C). The seed leaf is visible in 6 days and ready to transfer singly to 3½in (9cm) pots in 11 days. Handle only by the seed leaf not the stem. Give good light.
Varieties: Red Alert, fruits 1in (2½cm) diameter, prolific, very early. Sleaford Abundance, fruits slightly larger, heavy cropping. Minibel, 1½–2in (3–5cm) diameter. A more upright type. New varieties appear every year. Make sure yours is a dwarf, outdoor variety.

The tomato plants suitable for containers are dwarf outdoor varieties which grow naturally bushy with a tendency to trail. In a tub, urn or hanging basket they will stand considerable buffeting from wind and rain and still produce an abundance of ripe fruits.

Yellow pinpoint spots on foliage, tiny insects under leaves, later, webs. Red spider mite. Will increase rapidly if not treated. Spray with liquid derris and repeat every 10 days until clear. Do not pick fruit to eat after spraying without reading instructions on bottle.

Pale yellow blotches on leaf surfaces, brown snuff-like mould on undersides. Cladosporium disease. More common on tomatoes grown indoors. Spray with bordeaux mixture or ipridione and repeat every 10 days for rest of season.

Brown edges to leaves, dark, sunken marks on fruit. Potato blight. Usually occurs from midsummer on, after a wet, humid period. Spray with bordeaux mixture or ipridione and repeat every 10 days for rest of season. Do not spray with water if humid.

Plant wilts suddenly, brown canker at base of stem. Possibly also brown spots on leaves and fruit. Didymella stem rot. Remove affected plant, avoiding other plants. Burn if possible. Treat remaining plants with fungicide. At end of season, sterilize tub before renewing compost.

Young plants just taken out of doors have blackened, shrivelled edges to leaves. Put out too early. Introduce to outside in stages or protect in cold frame. If plant turns black in autumn, frost damage. Protect against frosts if fruit still to ripen.

Seedlings
1. *Seedlings grow tall, thin and straggly.* Too dark. Need full light in early spring.
2. *Stems damaged.* Bad handling. Always handle by leaves, not stems.
3. *Small seedlings collapse, base of stem cotton-like strands.* Damping off disease (pythium or phytophthora). Discard affected plants and treat rest with bordeaux mixture or copper fungicide. Keep seedlings in well ventilated place.
4. *Leaves yellow with blue-black undersides.* Roots grey and cotton-like. Overwatered. Discard. Resow if time or purchase young plants ready to go outside.

what goes wrong

Fruit does not ripen. Reduce water supply to keep soil nearly dry by early autumn.

Top of ripe fruit remains very hard and deep yellow. Too much nitrogen in feed. Fertilizer should be 1 part nitrogen to 3 parts potash. Use special tomato fertilizer only.

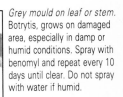

Grey mould on leaf or stem. Botrytis, grows on damaged area, especially in damp or humid conditions. Spray with benomyl and repeat every 10 days until clear. Do not spray with water if humid.

Ghost spots on fruit. Botrytis, caused by spores of mould settling on fruit from another source. Examine plant carefully for grey mould. Spray whole plant with diluted benomyl and repeat every 10 days until clear.

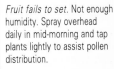

Fruit fails to set. Not enough humidity. Spray overhead daily in mid-morning and tap plants lightly to assist pollen distribution.

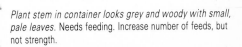

Plant stem in container looks grey and woody with small, pale leaves. Needs feeding. Increase number of feeds, but not strength.

Nemesia

Nemesia comes from South Africa and is an easily grown annual suitable for all kinds of containers. It goes well, for example, with a newly planted evergreen which needs space around it to grow but looks rather bare at first. Its only drawback when used in a planting scheme is that it finishes flowering by midsummer, so needs replacing with other plants later on. Or, if cut down to 3in (8cm) after flowering, it will produce a second crop of blooms.

Light: Seedlings indoors, full light. Plants outside, full sun.

Temperature: Germination, 50–65°F (10–18°C). Down to 40°F (4°C) outside but protect from frost.

Water: Water seedlings sparingly but do not allow to dry out. For mature plants, keep compost just moist.

Humidity: Dry. Do not spray or water overhead when in flower.

Soil: Good texture, free draining. Use loam-based No.1 or soil-less potting compost.

Feeding: Start 3 weeks after planting out, diluting liquid fertilizer to half maker's recommended strength. Feed every 10 days in soil, every 5 in soil-less. Increase to maker's recommended strength only if plants stop growing well.

Propagation: Sow from early spring to early summer on well drained seedling compost, covering with dust of fine dry compost. Keep between 50–65°F (10–18°C) and when seedlings appear after 4 days, move to full light. They soon grow too long and collapse in poor light. Prick out when large enough to handle. Plant out when frosts finished.

Tidying: Remove yellow leaves and flowers dropped onto leaves.

Varieties: Carnival has the largest flowers, Triumph a wider colour range.

Nemesia flowers come in a wide range of colours in warm tones of white, yellow, orange, red and brown. The plants grow about 12in (30cm) high and give a splash of colour from early summer.

Pale spots on leaves when in seed trays. Leaf spot fungus. Treat with bordeaux mixture to manufacturer's directions. Keep foliage dry especially at night.

Seedlings collapse, stems thread-like at base. Pythium disease. Nemesia is very susceptible if not in good light and sterile conditions. This includes water supply to seedlings. Remove affected plants and water soil with soil fungicide.

Seedlings die. Possibly alternaria on seed responsible. Always purchase good quality seed from a reliable source.

what goes wrong

Plant tall and weak. Too dark or was crowded in seed tray earlier. Give plenty of room for lateral development when pricking out into seed trays. Plants need full light and sun.

Cutting down.

Cut stems down to 3in (8cm) above soil level after flowering, using sharp scissors. Add a light top dressing of dry fertilizer to container to help plant produce new leaves and flowers.

Grey fluffy mould on leaves. Botrytis. On young plants, water left on leaves overnight or planted too close together. Water in the morning. On older plants, mould, encouraged if dead fallen flowers not removed from leaves. Pick off dead flowers and leaves.

Flowers rot. Sprayed with water or heavy rain. Do not spray or water overhead when in flower.

Frothy white deposit especially where leaf joins stem. Frog hopper, a sap sucking insect hiding in the froth. Wash off with diluted insecticide or jet of water or pick off by hand.

Clusters of small insects on foliage of young plants. Aphid. Spray with insecticide and repeat in 14 days if not clean. Older plants are less susceptible.

Bottom of stem turns black, foliage yellows. Phytophthora root and stem rot from contaminated water or soil. Plant unlikely to survive, so remove and treat soil with a fungicide.

Young or mature plants eaten at edges of leaves. Slugs or snails. Slugs likely to be hiding under seed tray. Snails under stones etc. Remove visible pests and put down slug pellets following maker's instructions. Keep away from pets and fishponds.

Plant wilts. Too dry. Keep soil just moist. Check daily in hot weather.

Plant collapses though still green. May be eaten off at ground level by cutworm. This will only occur if compost in container was not sterilized. Search through top 1in (2½cm) of soil surface. If not found, suspect slug and put down pellets as maker recommends.

Nicotiana

Tobacco plant

The sweet-scented Tobacco plant comes from South America and is of the same family as smoking tobacco. The scent of some varieties can be quite heady on a humid evening but the search for new colours has resulted in less perfume for others. They need a sunny spot and must always be protected from frost, however carefully they have been weaned to outside conditions.

Light: Maximum indoors and out.
Temperature: Germination, 65°F (18°C). No frost.
Water: Keep moist but not saturated.
Humidity: Dry when in flower. Spray after hot day (70°F, 21°C), especially when first planted out.
Soil: Loam-based No.3 or soil-less potting compost.
Feeding: Start when plants are outside but not planted into final containers. Feed every 2 weeks diluting to half maker's recommended strength. Two weeks after final planting start feeding every 10 days in soil, every 5 in soil-less, at maker's full recommended strength.
Propagation: Sow in mid-spring on prepared seedling compost. Do not cover seed with compost but place tray in plastic bag and cover with thick paper. Germination takes 4–5 days. Then give full light but not direct sun. Prick out when large enough to handle, leaving 3in (8cm) between plants. Will take full sun when growing.
Tidying: Remove whole flowering stem near base when flowers have died. This prevents seed pods forming so more flowers are produced.
Varieties: For patio and balcony, Affinis, white, highly scented. Crimson bedder, crimson 20in (50cm). For window boxes, Nikki series, many colours, 10in (25cm).

The varieties of sweet-scented Tobacco plant suitable for containers are usually 10–15 (25–38cm) high with colours including lime, pink, red and white. The taller white variety (affinis) is highly scented but its flowers close partially by day, opening towards evening.

Plant stops growing, soil surface dark and sickly. Waterlogged. Stop watering and check container drainage. Do not water again till almost dry.

Edges of leaves brown and shrivelled. Insecticide spray in bright sunshine or at too strong a concentration has scorched roots. Never use more than maker's recommended strength. Spray only in evening.

Early leaves have lacy holes where touching compost. Sciarid fly larvae. Drench compost with diluted malathion to maker's instructions. Rinse leaves in clear water to remove concentrated insecticide. This could cause scorch.

what goes wrong

Pale green/yellow mottling on leaves, twisted or knobbly stem. Virus disease. If severe, remove plant from container and destroy. If attack not too severe, flowering may continue to end of season. The presence of aphid on plants probably means that all will show symptoms.

Young plants in trays start to produce flower stems while still quite small, leaves are grey/green. Needs feeding. Feed at once It is better that flower stems do not develop until planting out when roots have a full 'run'. This will not apply if plants are in large pots before going outside.

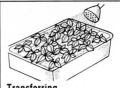

Transferring

1. Water tray well and drain. Tap end of tray on ground, hold open hand in front of plants and tilt box forward. Plants will lean away from box so whole contents can be lifted out.

2. Gently pull roots apart, leaving as much soil as possible around them, and plant singly in container.

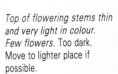

Green/brown winged flies inside flowers and under leaves. Aphid. Spray with diluted malathion to maker's instructions.

Top of flowering stems thin and very light in colour. Few flowers. Too dark. Move to lighter place if possible.

Flower stems hard and woody to the touch. Needs feeding. Feed once a week for 2 weeks with a high nitrogen feed then feed regularly.

Holes in leaves and leaf edges eaten away. Slugs or snails. Place slug pellets around to maker's recommendations. Keep away from pets and fishponds.

Plant turns black. Frost damage. Always protect from frost in early summer.

Leaves are grey green and small. Too dry. Water container and keep always moist but not soggy.

Plant leans over. Root rot from unsterile soil or overwatering. Stop watering, plant may recover. If plant turns yellow, remove.

Geranium

Both Zonal and Ivy-leaved Pelargoniums are suitable for outdoor planting, though they can also be grown successfully indoors on a sunny windowsill. All should be taken inside over winter and kept cool, dry and in good light until the following spring.

Light: Seedlings, good light indoors; cuttings shade while rooting. Mature plants, good light. Dappled shade suitable.

Temperature: Germination, 70°F (21°C) or more. Cuttings indoors need bottom heat of 65°F (18°C). Harden off gradually. No frost.

Water: Use tap, not stored water. Allow container to dry out between waterings.

Humidity: Dry, no overhead spraying.

Soil: Soil-less for germination and cuttings. Then loam-based No.2 or soil-less potting compost.

Feeding: Use liquid fertilizer at half maker's recommended strength every week in soil, every 3 days in soil-less. Increase strength to full recommended rate when plants are growing well outside.

Propagation: Take cuttings outdoors in midsummer or early autumn, indoors in early autumn and early spring. Root 3-4 to a 4in (10cm) pot, giving bottom heat of 65°F (18°C) for indoor cuttings. Sow seeds in early autumn or early spring. Clip pointed ends before sowing and sow in moist compost at 70°F (21°C) or more.

Tidying: Remove dead flower stems where they join main stem. Do not leave end of stem protruding.

Varieties: From seed, Caprice, coral pink. Sprinter, scarlet. Ringo, red. Playboy, mixed, bronze leaf, small flowers. From cuttings, Paul Crampel, single scarlet. Irene, semi-double cerise. Gustav Emich, red, double. Springtime, salmon, double. Treasure chest, orange red, double.

Geraniums have few equals for brilliance of colour and long-lasting blooms and are probably the most familiar of all windowbox and balcony plants. Flowers range from white through pink to brilliant scarlet and plants can be from 6 to 30in (15 to 75cm) tall.

what goes wrong

Holes appear in buds and leaves. Caterpillar. Search for and destroy pest. Dust carefully with gamma-BHC. A whole month's flowers may be eaten in a single night.

Plant suddenly goes yellow and sick. Black leg (pythium) from unsterile, overwatered soil. No cure. Take plant carefully from container and soak area with cheshunt compound or Jeyes fluid diluted to manufacturer's instructions.

Plant has yellow edge to bottom leaves. Leaves and flowers becoming smaller. Needs feeding. Increase number of liquid feeds per week. Do not increase strength.

Preparing a cutting

1. Choose shoot with at least 2 pairs of leaves and growing point and cut below second pair of leaves (about 4in, 10cm long).

2. Trim end to just below leaf and remove lowest pair of leaves. Dip cut end in rooting powder and insert round edge of pot, in seedling compost.

Many lush leaves but no flowers or only small ones. Overfeeding. Feed with half-strength fertilizer when plants young, increasing to full recommended strength as plant matures.

Plant does not grow well: no flowers. Too dark. Move to lighter place, full sun if possible. Or, sciarid fly larvae on roots. Drench soil with diluted malathion to maker's instructions.

Pinpoint white/pale yellow spots on surface of leaf, leaves look mealy underneath. Red spider mite. Spray plant with dimethoate or liquid derris and repeat until growth is a fresh green.

Grey mould on spent flower heads. Botrytis. This will occur after rain followed by humid conditions or spraying whole plant regularly. Remove heads very carefully to prevent spores from spreading and spray with benomyl.

Distorted flower buds or tender young growth. Aphid damage. Spray with pirimicarb or derris to maker's instructions.

Light yellow spots on top of foliage, increasing in size, and brown snuff-like powder on the underside. Pelargonium rust. Spray with dinocap fungicide.

Leaves redden when first planted outside in spring. Due to sudden chill after being protected. Transfer from inside to outside conditions must be gradual.

Leaves begin to yellow from base. Too dry. Increase water slightly but do not allow to become waterlogged.

Plant does not look fresh, soil is dark and sickly Poor drainage or overwatering. Make sure drainage is clear. Stop watering until dry.

Petunia

Petunias come from Argentina and are really half-hardy perennials though usually now grown as annuals. Few other plants flower so prolifically and they are ideal for the sheltered conditions usually given in containers. Flowers may be spoilt by rain but the actual plants recover quickly. As they will survive light frost they can be planted out early and will bloom from late spring through to late autumn. If buying plants, do not choose any with more than one flower showing.

Modern Petunias are compact, bushy plants from 12 to 18in (30–45cm) high. The bell-shaped flowers come in almost every colour of the spectrum including a recent yellow variety and some with two-coloured stripes.

Light: Seedlings need good light. Outdoors, full sun. No more than 20% shade.
Temperature: Germination, 65°F (18°C). Outside, will survive light frost. Best over 50°F (10°C).
Water: Allow container almost to dry out between waterings.
Humidity: Do not spray flowers.
Soil: Loam-based No. 1 or soil-less potting compost.
Feeding: Feed every 14 days in soil, starting 6 weeks after planting. In soil-less, feed weekly, starting 3 weeks after planting out. Liquid feed best, at half maker's recommended strength.
Propagation: In mid-spring, sow fine seed thinly in prepared tray. Do not cover with compost. Place in propagator or plastic bag at 65°F (18°C) in light shade, not full sun. Germination takes 8 days. Prick out seedlings as soon as large enough to handle, into small pots or 2in (5cm) apart in trays. Reduce to 50°F (10°C) and give maximum light. Will grow at 45°F (7°C) but slowly.
Tidying: Remove wet flowers after rain.
Varieties: Many hundreds. Multifloras have smaller flowers but are very prolific. Resisto Rose Pink most rainproof. Grandifloras have large flowers but are less weather-proof.

Growing from seed

1. Sow thinly in prepared, drained compost in seed. Place fine seed on palm of hand and tap edge with index finger of other hand so seed falls evenly. Do not cover seed with compost.

2. Place in propagator or plastic bag at 65°F (18°C). Shade from sun but do not keep completely dark.

3. When seeds germinate (8 days) remove propagator cover. Prick out singly when seedlings large enough to handle.

what goes wrong

Young plants grow slowly. Too cold. Plants will survive light frosts but grow better if above 50°F (10°C)

Leaves grow lush but few flowers appear. Overfeeding. Do not feed until plant has been in soil for 6 weeks, then feed regularly with half-strength liquid feed.

Plant wilts and droops. Too hot and dry. Water well but allow soil to dry out between waterings. Plant survives well in dry weather.

Young plant looks thin and weedy. Too dark. Move to lighter position with full sunlight.

Small winged green flies on leaves and inside flower. Leaves sticky. Aphid. Spray with systemic insecticide and repeat after 14 days if pest has returned.

Flowers turn colourless and soggy, all flowers affected. Heavy rain damage. Remove old blooms and new buds will soon open. Protect plants from heavy rain if possible.

White ghost spots on flowers. Alternaria disease. Spray with benomyl once.

Yellow blotches on leaves, dark patches on flower stems. Tobacco mosaic virus. No cure, but plant will not be badly affected. Sterilize container before planting more petunias or tobacco plants in it or disease will spread.

Plant turns yellow from base upwards, leaves look limp. Root rot from overwatering. Check drainage in container is clear and allow soil to dry out between waterings. Petunias prefer to be too dry rather than too wet.

Light brown streaks on leaf stems and plant stem, later turning black. Advanced stage of alternaria disease. Spray with benomyl or, if flowering finished, remove plants.

Primula elatior

Polyanthus

Polyanthus and primroses are well known signs of spring and though the flowering season is short, they are well worth an early place in boxes and tubs. It is preferable not to buy plants in flower in spring as they are difficult to establish. The true primrose *(Primula acaulis)* is of the same family as the Polyanthus and needs the same treatment.

Light: Maximum possible in spring. 40% shade in high summer when plants are resting or establishing themselves in a new place.

Temperature: Not above 55°F (13°C). Shade in summer. Will stand frost.

Water: Cool, moist soil. Flower buds drop off if soil too dry before flowering.

Humidity: Spray leaves in hot weather to help keep it cool.

Soil: Loam-based No. 3 or, better still, soilless potting compost.

Feeding: After flowering, put layer of fish, blood and bonemeal on top of container, as maker recommends. Do not feed from early autumn to later winter, then feed with fertilizer diluted to maker's recommended strength every 5 days until in full flower.

Propagation: Sow in late spring/early summer. Prepare seed tray and sow very thinly. Cover with ⅛in (2mm) moist compost, seal in plastic bag and keep in cool (45°F, 7°C), sunless place until germination (10–20 days). Compost should stay moist without watering. Prick out when large enough to handle into small pots or 2in (5cm) apart in trays. Or, divide existing plants after flowering.

Tidying: Cut off dead flowers. Remove dead leaves at the end of winter.

Varieties: Hardy, Giant Bouquet, Kelscott, Giant Yellow. Almost hardy, Pacific hybrids.

Polyanthus are 5–9in (13–23cm) at flowering stage with bright green leaves and flowers in a wide range of colours. The flowers are usually clustered on each stem, though single blooms on a stem, like the true primrose, are possible.

Flower buds damaged, may be eaten away completely. Birds, especially sparrows. May occur whenever buds visible but only one colour may be attacked. Tie black cotton thread on sticks 2in (5cm) above plant to prevent attack. Chemicals effective only for short periods.

Leaves droop, soil dark and sour. Waterlogged. Check drainage and water less often. Keep moist but not soaked.

Whole plant turns suddenly yellow and wilts. Root rot disease. Remove carefully from container and destroy. Water soil with fungicide, diluted as maker recommends.

what goes wrong

Division

1. After flowering, remove plant carefully from container and shake soil from around roots.

2. Gently pull roots and stems apart. Plant in shady part of garden or in pot and keep moist and cool through summer. Plant in position in mid-autumn. Remove dead bottom leaves in spring.

Divided crowns do not produce healthy green leaves by early autumn. Planted in hot sun or slug damage. Plant divided plants in shade and apply slug pellets monthly. Bottom leaves will shrivel naturally in late winter and should be removed.

Leaves and buds covered in tiny green insects. Aphid. Spray with diluted malathion or general insecticide. If attacked in autumn, buds and flowers may be distorted following spring. Spray monthly in summer to prevent attacks.

Edges of young leaves have dry, shrivelled patches in spring. Handled in frost. Do not touch frosted leaves.

Leaves almost hide flowers. Too dark or too hot in confined space. No cure but improve conditions next year.

Holes in leaves. Slugs or snails. Put down slug pellets as maker recommends but keep away from pets and fish ponds.

Leaves pale green with veins nearly white. Needs feeding. Feed every 5 days in spring while growing.

Flower buds drop. Too dry. Keep soil moist, especially when buds appear.

Fluffy grey mould in crown. Botrytis due to lack of air movement round plant. Remove decaying tissue and spray with benomyl and iprodione. Repeat after 10 days.

Salvia

Salvias come originally from Brazil and though naturally perennials, are quickly killed by frost; in countries with cold winters they are therefore best grown as annuals. Modern varieties seldom exceed 12in (30cm) high, so are ideal for windowboxes.

Light: Maximum possible at all times.
Temperature: Germination, 70°F (21°C). Young plants, 60°F (16°C). Outside, protect from cold winds. No frost.
Water: Keep moist, not waterlogged.
Humidity: Seedlings, young plants: light syringing. Stop when flowering.
Soil: Loam-based No.3 or soil-less potting. Even better, equal parts of both.
Feeding: Start feeding young plants while still in tray, using liquid fertilizer at half maker's recommended strength. Ten days after final planting, start feeding at full recommended strength every 10 days in soil, every 5 in soil-less.
Propagation: Cuttings are difficult to overwinter so seeds sown in mid-spring are better. Use soil-less potting compost and cover seed with ¼in (½cm) fine compost, pressed down lightly. Place in plastic bag and cover with thick paper. Keep at 70°F (21°C). After germination (7–10 days) put in full light. Prick out singly into 3½ (9cm) pots or in trays 3in (8cm) apart as soon as they can be handled (about 15 days after sowing). Keep at 70°F (21°C) for 1 more week, then 60°F (16°C) until put outside.
Tidying: Snap off dead flower spikes to encourage branching.
Varieties: Volcano, midgreen foliage, bright scarlet, dwarf, compact and early. Blaze of Fire, slightly taller than Volcano, vigorous, compact. Midget, very dwarf and early. Carabinierre, dark foliage, very strong, grows with large spike. Dress Parade, mixture of cream, salmon, pink, scarlet, purple.

Salvias are bushy plants 9–15 (23-38cm) tall and produce clusters of flowers in a pyramid-shaped spike. Flower buds show early and when buying, choose plants whose bud colour is visible but not advanced; the leaves should be a fresh green, going right down to the base of the stem.

Pinpoint yellow or white spots on leaves. Underside is mealy. Red spider mite. Spray with diluted malathion at 10 day intervals until completely clear.

Upper leaves and growing points show yellow and pale green markings. Sometimes occurs after a check in growth due to cold. Condition usually disappears when warm weather returns.

Grey mould appears on flowers or foliage. Botrytis. Carefully remove any affected parts to avoid dropping spores on other plants and then spray with benomyl.

Plant wilts in hot sunshine. Needs more water. Keep soil always moist. Leaves will turn yellow if left without water for too long.

Seedlings develop dark and shrivelled area around base. Pythium or other root and stem rots. Seedlings will not recover. Remove affected plants and those near them. Spray compost with soil fungicide. If time, sow again in sterile compost and use only tap water for watering and spraying.

Leaves turn black and plant collapses. Frost. Protect from frost in spring.

Pricking out
1. When seedlings are large enough to handle, remove carefully from seed tray, holding them by the seed leaves.

2. Prepare 3½ (9cm) pots or tray, with holes for planting seedlings. Plant each one singly in pot or 3in (8cm) apart in tray. Moisten compost and leave in shade for 2 days.

Small insects clustered round growing points, possibly inside flowers. Aphids. Spray with pirimicarb or diluted malathion. Pirimicarb will not harm bees.

what goes wrong

Flower stem distorted possibly with sunken area underneath flowers. Capsid bug. Spray with systemic insecticide.

Leaves have ragged holes, stem possibly rasped away. Slugs or snails. Place slug pellets as maker recommends.

Dark streaks and misshapen leaves. Virus. No action can be taken but flowering may not be affected. Destroy plants at end of season.

Bottom leaves turn yellow, upper leaves are grey/ green. Needs feeding. Increase number but not strength of feed.

Whole stem black, leaves yellow, flowers droop. Waterlogged. Check drainage. Plant will not recover. If others not yet affected allow soil to almost dry out before watering again. Yellow leaves also sign of dryness.

Silverleaf

The Silverleaf, a native of Southern Europe, is a perennial but as it becomes woody and rather straggly after its first year, it is usually grown as an annual. It can be grown from seed or cuttings, will stand moderate frosts and thrives in almost any type of soil.

Light: Full light. Shade cuttings until rooted.

Temperature: Germination, 55°F (13°C). Cuttings taken in midsummer need no extra heat. Protect from severe cold. Will stand moderate frost.

Water: Keep moist to dry.

Humidity: Dry, no spraying.

Soil: Any loam-based or soil-less compost. If plant kept for several years, add fresh compost for 3rd season.

Feeding: Feed every 14 days with liquid fertilizer diluted to maker's recommended strength.

Propagation: Sow seed in early spring, soon after days lengthen. Cover with enough compost to hide seed and keep at 55°F (13°C). Prick out when large enough to handle and keep in cool, airy room until putting outside in mid-spring. Plant in container by late spring. For cuttings, cut off non-flowering shoots about 3–4in (8–10cm) long in midsummer. Strip off lower pair of leaves, and dip end in rooting powder. Plant singly into small peat pots of seedling compost or place several round outside of 4in (11cm) pot, water well and leave in shady spot. Keep moist and rooting will occur in 3 weeks. Pot singly in 3½in (9cm) pots if rooted in groups and grow outdoors until late autumn, when they need protection.

Varieties: Silver Dust, very dwarf and finely cut leaves (6in, 15cm). Candicans (10in, 25cm). Diamond, broadly cut leaves (12in, 30cm). Heights are first year's growth. Mature height double.

The attractive silvery white foliage of the Silverleaf remains on the plant all year round, providing a foil for summer flowers and a patch of brightness in winter. Its own deep lemon yellow flowers appear in its second year.

Small green lice on young seedlings. Aphid. Spray once with diluted malathion or pirimicarb. A repeat attack is unlikely as plant gets older.

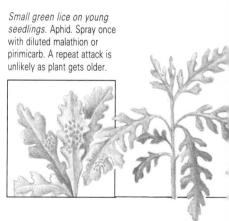

Leaves are dark grey/green instead of silvery white. In seedlings this is natural and colour will appear well before planting time. In older plants, over rich compost especially if feeding was regularly high in nitrogen. Feed with potash sulphate, watering well. Choose balanced feed in future.

what goes wrong

Changing the topsoil

If keeping from year to year, renew top 3in (7½cm) soil in container after 2nd winter. Carefully remove soil, teasing it from around roots. Add fresh compost, firming round roots. Water well.

Fine yellowish streaks in leaves. Thrips. Usually occurs during hot weather. Spray with diluted malathion during the evening and repeat after 14 days.

Small dark spots on leaves, especially on young seedlings. Leaf spot fungus, probably alternaria. This disease can be seed or air borne. Always buy treated seed. Spray with iprodione or bordeaux mixture.

Leaves have brown edges. Too concentrated feed or insecticide, or spraying insecticide in full sun in the heat of the day. If in winter, possibly frost scorch, in which case do not prune off affected stems until early spring. Spray only in early morning or evening; always follow instructions when feeding or spraying insecticides.

Leaves lose colour and plant wilts. Container too dry. Soak well and leave to drain to just moist before watering again.

Holes in foliage, flower buds eaten. Caterpillar. Pick off pest and dust carefully with gamma-BHC if badly infested. Keep away from vegetables.

Base of plant becomes brown and soggy, soil is scummy. Waterlogged. Senecios prefer moist/dry rather than moist/wet soil. Make sure drainage holes are clear and allow container to dry out before watering again.

Mature plant lies along the tub, especially when flower stems growing. Plant straggles naturally with age. Could be staked, or if unsightly, cut off flower stems.

67

Tagetes patula

French marigold

The marigold family are natives of Mexico and so luxuriate in hot conditions and do not need much moisture. Single flowered varieties are virtually unaffected by rain (and resistant to rain-induced diseases) but the double and larger flowered ones are soon damaged. All will succumb to the slightest frost. Two other Tagetes are commonly grown: *T. signata* is small flowered and dwarf; *T. erecta*, the African marigold, is taller with large double flowers. Except for its very dwarf varieties, it is not suitable for window-boxes.

French marigolds are bushy plants about 10in (25cm) high. The flowers, from 1½–2in (4–5cm) across, are almost always yellow or orange but may have red or maroon markings. They are single or double according to variety.

Light: Maximum. Can stand 20% shade if light brilliant for rest of day.
Temperature: Indoors light and air more important than warmth. Outside, choose sheltered area. No frost.
Water: Seedlings, just moist. For mature plants, soak container thoroughly and re-water only when soil nearly dry.
Humidity: Dry. Do not spray double flowers or they may rot.
Soil: Loam-based No. 1.
Feeding: Monthly with liquid fertilizer at half maker's recommended strength; or plant sticks.
Propagation: Seed is large and easy to grow. Sow in prepared seed tray in early spring. Cover with compost and keep at 60°F (16°C). Germination takes 3 days. Prick off singly into small pots or trays not more than 10 days after sowing. Give maximum light and air. Plant out after frost has finished.
Tidying: Snap off dead heads to encourage more flowers.
Varieties: Single, Cinnabar, orange, gold. Pascal, Susie Wong, Ruffled Red. Double: Golden Ball, Orange Beauty, Queen Sophia, Gold and Boy series.

Holes in buds and leaves. Caterpillar damage. Pick off pest and spray plant with liquid derris or dust with derris dust. Inspect regularly.

Buds puckered, leaves distorted. Aphid. Spray with insecticide. Repeat 10 days later if pest persists.

Plant wilts slightly but stays green. Slug attacking main stem. Place slug pellets around as maker's instructions. Keep away from pets and fishponds. Stake plant until recovered.

Plant wilts and droops. Too hot and dry. Water well, soaking container to bottom but allow soil to dry out before watering again.

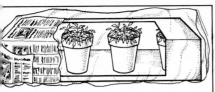

Protection

French marigolds will die if frosted so protect young plants at night when frost expected. If in cold frame, close lid and wrap with hessian or newspaper and sheet of plastic. If no frame, cover with cardboard box, with newspapers and plastic as extra protection.

Plant turns black and collapses. Frost damage. Plant will not survive frost so protect young plants in spring. Remove dead plant from container.

Leaves lush and healthy but few flowers. Soil too rich or fed too often. Feed once a month with half-strength fertilizer or use plant sticks.

Plant does not grow bushy or produce flowers. Soil too rich or fed too often. Feed monthly with fertilizer at half maker's recommended strength or use plant sticks.

Pinpoint white markings on leaf surface, underside mealy and pinkish-grey. Webs. Red spider mite. Spray with dimethoate or use liquid derris as maker recommends.

what goes wrong

Double flowers turn brown and rot. Water damage. Do not spray or water overhead large-flowered types. Protect from heavy rain.

Leaves turn yellow and droop. Too wet, overwatered. Allow soil to dry out between waterings and keep plant in sunny position.

One branch hangs limp, rest healthy. Botrytis where branch joins main stem. Cut off affected branch cleanly and treat rest of plant with benomyl.

Plant turns yellow from base. Phytophthora root rot. Remove affected plant and treat all plants in container with cheshunt compound.

Thunbergia alata

Black-eyed Susan

The Black-eyed Susan is a native of Africa and will not survive frost. However, once the danger of frost has passed, it can be planted out into containers and will climb a balcony rail or trellis or trail attractively from a tub. Cuttings taken in summer can be overwintered indoors: a cool, double-glazed window ledge is ideal. Do not leave taking cuttings too late in the season as the parent plant will be destroyed by frost at the beginning of autumn. Though tender, the plant is not especially affected by pests and diseases.

Light: Bright, especially indoors.
Temperature: Germination, 65–70°F (18–21°C). Outside, 50–90°F (10–32°C). Protect from strong winds.
Water: Do not overwater. A plant drooping from dryness will quickly recover when watered.
Humidity: Light spray after hot day (over 75°F, 24°C). Use clean water or flowers will mark.
Feeding: Every 10 days in loam, every 5 in soil-less. Dilute as maker recommends.
Soil: Loam-based No. 2 or soil-less potting compost.
Propagation: Sow seed in early spring, in prepared seed tray. Cover with ⅛in (2mm) dry compost and place in propagator or plastic bag at 65–70°F (18–21°C). Prick off singly into small pots when large enough to handle and grow in light. In late spring start to harden off, putting outside in sheltered spot by day, indoors at night. After 1 week, leave outside overnight in cold frame or under cardboard box covered with thick, dry material whenever frost threatens. Or, take cuttings in summer.
Tidying: Remove yellow leaves.
Varieties: Alata, creamy yellow. Gibsonii, deep orange.

The Black-eyed Susan is a trailing, twining plant with thin, wiry stems which can reach 4ft (over 1m) in ideal condition. The deep creamy yellow flowers have a round 'eye' of such deep purple it looks black and are followed by seed pods like miniature Chinese lanterns.

Growing point distorted with clusters of small insects. Dark sooty, sticky deposit on leaves. Aphid. Spray with diluted general insecticide according to maker's instructions.

Taking cuttings

1. In midsummer take cutting 4in (10cm) long from tip of shoot, just below pair of leaves. Remove lowest leaves and dip bottom ½in (12mm) in hardwood rooting compound.

2. Insert 1in (2½cm) into pot of seedling compost. Water and keep at 70°F (21°C) until rooted. Keep cool (45–50°F, 7–10°C) indoors in winter, treating as seedling next spring.

Leaves pale, new leaves small. Needs feeding. Feed every 10 days in loam, every in soil-less compost. Do not increase strength of feed.

what goes wrong

Leaves turn yellow. Too dry or needs feeding. Check conditions. Water if soil dry. If soil correct, feed regularly. Do not increase strength of feed.

Few flowers, hidden by leaves. Too dark. Move to lighter place.

Leaves purple at edges. Cold winds. Will recover if weather improves. If cold continues, move to sheltered place if possible.

Flowers brown on edge of petal. Insecticide sprayed in sun. Spray only in dull, still weather or in evening. Or, too strong mixture. Follow maker's instructions. Severe scorching may kill plant.

Leaves turn black and soggy. Frost damage. Protect young plants in late spring and early autumn. Remove dead plants.

Flowers lose brightness and leaves look dull. Too hot. Spray in evening.

Flowers marked with brown spots. Sprayed with dirty water. Make sure water for spraying is clean.

Leaves grey and brittle with pinpoint white spots above, pinkish-grey underneath. Red spider mite. Spray with liquid derris or systemic insecticide every 10 days until new growth is green again.

Plant droops. Too dry or waterlogged. Check soil. If dry, water at once and plant will recover. If wet, check drainage holes and allow soil to dry out before watering again.

71

Nasturtium

The Nasturtium is a fast-growing climbing or trailing plant, a native of South America. With its gaudy coloured flowers it gives a brilliant display at little cost. If you do not require a climber, the similar *Nasturtium nana* is a dwarf, more bushy species, while for covering a trellis the even faster-growing *Tropaeoleum canariense* (Canary creeper) with its bright yellow flowers is superb. All three plants need the same basic treatment.

Light: Maximum. Sunshine essential for lots of flowers.

Temperature: Germination, 45°F (7°C). No frost. Will stand hot conditions well.

Water: A sappy plant which needs moisture in soil; keep container moist.

Humidity: Dry air, no spraying.

Feeding: Once a month at maker's recommended strength. More frequent feeding leads to lush leaves but few flowers.

Soil: Loam-based No. 1.

Propagation: Sow pea-sized seeds direct into container loam 1in (24mm) deep in late spring. Water compost 24 hours beforehand and allow to drain. Allow 6 seeds to a 12in (30cm) diameter tub or 16 to a 4ft (120cm) trough and thin to 3 and 8 seedlings respectively. Number of seeds for other sized containers can be worked out from this. Or sow indoors individually in small pots in mid-spring, moving to cold frame when 3in (7cm) high. Plant out in early summer.

Tidying: Cut off dead flowers once a week. This prolongs flowering.

Varieties: Gleam hybrids, trailing. Tom Thumb, compact. The smallest varieties grow to only 6in (15cm) so are suitable for windowboxes as well as larger containers. Choose a variety which suits your situation. *Tropaeoleum canariense* is always a climber or trailer.

Nasturtiums have almost white stems and brilliant green leaves with contrasting paler veins. Some, like these, have variegated leaves. The flowers, about 3in (7cm) across, range from pale yellow through gold, orange and scarlet to a rusty brown-red. Sun lovers, they produce lush leaves but few flowers if kept in shade.

Holes in leaves and flowers. Caterpillar damage. Caterpillars eat away buds, flowers and stem. Pick off all you can find and spray with derris or dust with derris powder. Ragged flowers may have been eaten by earwigs hidden inside flowers or between box and sill. Spray with diluted malathion and remove debris where pest may hide.

Grey powdery deposit on stems and leaf stalks. Powdery mildew. This may retard growth and should be sprayed as soon as noticed with copper-based fungicide, diluted to maker's instructions.

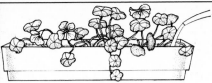

Watering

Nasturtiums need moist soil but make sure container is well drained. Check surface of soil daily in hot weather and if it feels dry and crumbly, add water. If it becomes heavy and does not dry in cold weather, check drainage holes and allow container to dry out before watering again.

Plant collapses, leaves turn black. Frost damage. Plant will not survive frost. Protect your plants until danger of frost is over. Remove plants at end of summer season.

Very large lush leaves and few flowers. Soil too rich. Do not feed for at least a month, then feed only once a month.

Flowers under leaves and hardly visible. Plant in too much shade. Mover to sunnier position. Needs full sunshine whenever possible.

what goes wrong

Leaves turning yellow over all plant. Soil too wet and cold. Allow to dry out before watering again and check drainage layer in container is not blocked or container standing in water.

Stems crinkled and rubbery at soil level. Stem rot. Soil probably waterlogged from poor drainage. Spray stems with benomyl and improve drainage in container.

Black, sappy looking flies in clusters on plant; plant turning black. Black aphid. Spray with diluted malathion or rub aphids between fingers to kill them. If no insecticide, spray with diluted detergent.

White wriggly lines on leaves. Leaf miner grubs inside leaf tissue. Press grub at end of trail between finger and thumb or spray with diluted systemic insecticide.

Flower buds and growing tips of stems distorted. Aphid. Spray with general insecticide and repeat after 10 days.

73

Verbena hybrida

Verbena

Verbenas grow on average 12–14in (30-45cm) in height and through recent breeding work are becoming more bushy, less straggling plants. They are not easy to grow from seed and seedlings emerge erratically. To avoid root disturbance at planting out time, prick them out into individual pots so that the roots can be planted intact. If buying plants, try to find those grown in this way, not crowded all together in a tray.

Light: A sunny spot. Needs maximum light.
Temperature: Germination, 70°F (21°C). As soon as seedlings appear, 65°F (18°C). One week after pricking out, 55°F (13°C). Keep out of draughts. No frost.
Water: Soak container thoroughly, then allow to dry out before watering but do not leave dry for too long. Good drainage essential.
Humidity: Dislikes high humidity. Keep in airy place while indoors.
Soil: Gritty, loam-based No. 2 or soil-less potting compost.
Feeding: Start 2 weeks after planting in final container, then every 10 days in soil, every 5 in soil-less. Use liquid fertilizer at maker's recommended strength.
Propagation: Sow seeds as soon as days start to lengthen on well moistened seedling compost. Cover with ⅛in (2mm) compost and keep moist so hard seed coat softens. Place in propagator at 70°F (21°C) and cover. Bring tray into light when first seedlings appear (about 1 week). Prick out when large enough to handle into individual pots.
Tidying: Remove seed heads after flowers have died.
Varieties: Royal Bouquet, upright, good colours with white 'eye'. Derby Salmon, Derby Scarlet, both bushy, no 'eye'. Tropic, slightly taller.

Verbena's small flowers are grouped at the top of a flower stem and open gradually to form an elongated head of brilliant colours, from white, pale pink to red and from pale blue to deep purple. Flowering season lasts without a break from early summer to late autumn.

New leaves small and pale, slow growth. Needs feeding. Use liquid fertilizer every 10 days at recommended strength.

Young plants stop growing. Examine soil surface for tiny almost transparent grubs, larvae of mushroom fly, feeding on roots. Water soil with malathion diluted to maker's instructions. (Small black flies may also be seen on surface.)

Newly potted seedlings fall over and stem near compost thin and soft. Pythium or damping off disease. Remove affected seedlings and those near them and water soil with fungicide. Never water young seedlings from a rain butt; tap water is safe.

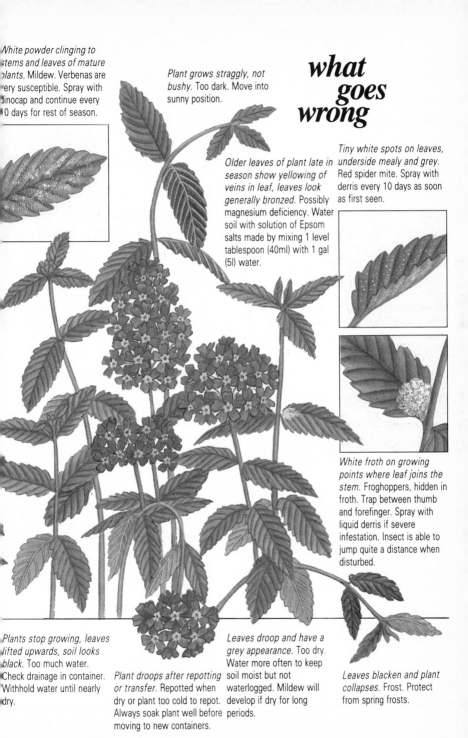

White powder clinging to stems and leaves of mature plants. Mildew. Verbenas are very susceptible. Spray with dinocap and continue every 10 days for rest of season.

Plant grows straggly, not bushy. Too dark. Move into sunny position.

what goes wrong

Older leaves of plant late in season show yellowing of veins in leaf, leaves look generally bronzed. Possibly magnesium deficiency. Water soil with solution of Epsom salts made by mixing 1 level tablespoon (40ml) with 1 gal (5l) water.

Tiny white spots on leaves, underside mealy and grey. Red spider mite. Spray with derris every 10 days as soon as first seen.

White froth on growing points where leaf joins the stem. Froghoppers, hidden in froth. Trap between thumb and forefinger. Spray with liquid derris if severe infestation. Insect is able to jump quite a distance when disturbed.

Plants stop growing, leaves lifted upwards, soil looks black. Too much water. Check drainage in container. Withhold water until nearly dry.

Plant droops after repotting or transfer. Repotted when dry or plant too cold to repot. Always soak plant well before moving to new containers.

Leaves droop and have a grey appearance. Too dry. Water more often to keep soil moist but not waterlogged. Mildew will develop if dry for long periods.

Leaves blacken and plant collapses. Frost. Protect from spring frosts.

Viola tricolor

Pansy

Pansies are totally hardy in a temperate climate and produce flowers from late winter to the end of summer. Being small (4–6in, 10–15cm) they are ideal for windowboxes or small containers. They are easily raised from seed and grow best in dappled shade, not in hot, dry positions. Buy plants that are short and bushy with deep green leaves. If they already have open flowers they will be difficult to establish.

Light: In summer, dappled shade or half shade, half sun. In autumn, winter and early spring, full light.
Temperature: Germination, 50°F (10°C). Cool and airy while growing. Will stand frost.
Water: Keep soil moist.
Soil: Rich, fibrous soil. Loam-based No. 3 with ⅓ coarse peat added or soil-less compost based on coarse sphagnum peat.
Feeding: Feed every week in soil, every 4 days in soil-less, using liquid fertilizer diluted to maker's recommended strength.
Propagation: Sow thinly in early spring or midsummer in prepared seed tray. Cover seed lightly with dry compost and cover tray with thick paper. Keep at 50°F (10°C). Prick out singly into 3½in (9cm) pots or 2in (5cm) apart in seed trays. Water well and keep shaded for 2 days. If indoors, place in light window but not full sunlight. Outside, keep out of summer sun. Or, take cuttings.
Tidying: Pick off seed pods to encourage more flowers to grow.
Varieties: Celestial Queen, lavender and Orion, yellow, will flower in late winter from midsummer sowing. Swiss Giants, Majestic Giants, Imperial Orange, Prince, and Sunny Boy all have 'marked' flowers. Paramount Azure Blue, Golden Crown and all the Dream Strain colours are clear of the dark marking.

The garden Pansy's flat flowers are made up of 5 overlapping petals which form a near circle. The most popular are those with a dark marking resembling a face but a range of self-coloured hybrids is also available.

Spots on leaves. Either ramularia or phillosticta, both leaf-spotting fungi, encouraged by too high humidity. Spray with a general fungicide and try to improve air circulation around plants.

Holes in leaves and eaten areas on stems. Slugs or snails. Scatter slug pellets round following maker's instructions. Keep away from pets and fishponds. Slugs will feed off the roots of the pansy throughout the winter if not checked. When weather is mild and damp, place a few pellets around and look out for slime trails.

Plant becomes yellow and falls over. Phytophthora root disease. No cure at this stage. Remove carefully and drench soil with cheshunt compound. Treat roots and stems of any other pansies in container.

Cuttings

1. In spring or summer cut off non-flowering shoot just below a leaf joint, not more than 3in (8cm) long.

2. Remove lowest leaf and dip cut end of stem in rooting powder.

3. Insert cuttings round edge of 3½in (9cm) pot so that lowest leaf is level with compost.

4. Keep moist and cool. Pot separately in 3½in (9cm) pots after 2–3 weeks, when rooted.

what goes wrong

Opening flowers chewed and buds also damaged. Earwigs, in leaves or under debris during day, come out to feed at night. Clear up debris and spray with gamma-BHC or diluted malathion to maker's instructions. Gamma-BHC will taint food crops.

Foliage turns pale green and new flowers are smaller. Needs feeding. If feeding regular, was compost good quality? Top dress container with fresh compost.

Plant becomes yellow and looks distorted. Root aphid. Spray with diluted malathion.

Powdery deposit on stems and/or leaves. Powdery mildew. This can be made worse by keeping plant too dry. Spray with benomyl or iprodione. Keep soil moist.

Buds drop before opening. Too dry at root. Keep soil moist always.

Blotches of yellow on top of foliage with brown pustules on the underside. Pansy rust. This will gradually reduce flowering and plant will be unsightly. Spray with dinocap fungicide.

Plant wilts and droops. Needs watering. Do not allow to dry out completely in hot sunshine.

Small insects on leaves, growing points small. Aphids. Spray with diluted malathion or derris following maker's instructions. Repeat in one week. Pansy is very susceptible.

Plant grows weak and straggly. Too hot while developing. Keep seedlings cool until they are well established with leaves and buds beginning to develop.

Zinnia

Zinnias come from Mexico and so are not suitable for a cold, windy position or one shaded by trees or buildings for much of the day. They grow rapidly and seeds should not be sown before mid-spring or the plants may be ready to put outside before it is warm enough for them. Do not try to check their natural growth or they may become diseased.

Light: Maximum at all times.
Temperature: Germination, 65–70°F (18–21°C). Seedlings, 55°F (13°C). No frost.
Water: Keep soil always just moist. Never overwater.
Humidity: Keep dry, do not spray or water overhead when in flower.
Soil: Rich, well-drained. Loam-based No. 3 or soil-less potting compost.
Feeding: In loam-based No. 3, start 3–4 weeks after planting out, using liquid fertilizer at maker's recommended strength, then feed every 10 days. Feed soilless 10 days after planting out, then every 5 days.
Propagation: Sow seed thinly in mid-spring in drained soil-less seedling compost. Cover with ¼in (6mm) compost and lightly press with flat board. Do not place in plastic bag but cover tray with thick paper and place in propagator at 65–70°F (18–21°C). Germination takes 2 days. Remove paper immediately and place tray in light, airy room with no draughts. Prick out 2in (5cm) apart within 2–3 days and start to harden off when plants about 5in (12cm) tall. Do not put outside until all danger of frost passed.
Tidying: Remove dead flowers.
Varieties: Goblin, Lilliput, Pumila and Peter Pan are all good dwarf windowbox varieties. Giant Dahlia Flowered, Giants of California, Tetra State Fair, very large flowers for patio and balcony. Mixed colours.

Zinnia flowers measure up to 5in (13cm) across, in colours ranging from white to yellow, rose, scarlet and violet. They are long lasting when cut but need bright light and a sunny position to flourish.

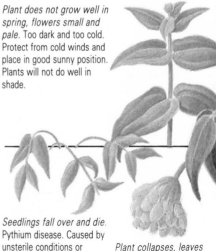

Plant does not grow well in spring, flowers small and pale. Too dark and too cold. Protect from cold winds and place in good sunny position. Plants will not do well in shade.

Seedlings fall over and die. Pythium disease. Caused by unsterile conditions or contaminated water. Never use stored water for seedlings. Remove affected seedlings and those around them. Water soil with fungicide.

Plant collapses, leaves black. Frost. Protect from frost in spring.

what goes wrong

Buds and flowers malformed, often tilted to one side. Leaves tattered. Capsid bug. Spray with insecticide every 10 days until early autumn. Do not use malathion which may cause leaf scorching.

Flower petals have ragged edges and small holes. Earwigs, hidden between windowbox and sill or under decaying leaves. Dust plant carefully with gamma-BHC or set trap by putting a little dried grass or straw in a jar, supporting it upside down on a small cane. Next morning many of these pests will have installed themselves in the new home. They can then be destroyed by emptying into boiling water.

Grey spots on flowers and brown edges. Flower scorch fungus, occurs in a humid season. Spray with bordeaux mixture or iprodione. If flowers are spotted without brown edges disease is likely to be botrytis but treatment is the same.

Foliage pales, new flowers smaller. Needs feeding. Feed more often with fertilizer diluted to manufacturer's recommendation. Do not increase strength.

White or grey fluffy mould on stems. Stem turns brown. Botrytis well developed. Zinnia is highly susceptible. Carefully cut off all affected parts of the plant, avoiding sharp movements if possible as spores disperse easily. Spray with a fungicide and continue every week or 10 days for the rest of season.

Clusters of small insects round bud. Aphid. Spray with insecticide. Do not use malathion.

Mottled leaves with yellow rings, distorted growth. Spotted wilt virus. No cure. Destroy plant.

Bottom of stem blackened. Plant is sickly. Phytophthora stem and root rot. Caused by unsterilized soil or contaminated water. No cure. Remove and treat soil with a fungicide.

Plant looks yellow and sickly, possibly with mould at base of stem. Soil is dark and sour. Overwatered. Check drainage in container and allow to dry out before watering again.

Young plants, especially soon after moving out of doors, develop small spots, enlarging to circles. Alternaria disease. It can be seed or airborne. Spray plant with bordeaux mixture. White spots may also be caused by chemical spray or hail.

Stems of plants eaten off at ground level. Slugs or snails if slimy trail present on soil, container or ground. Otherwise suspect cutworm. Put down slug bait as maker recommends. Keep away from pets and fishponds. For cutworm spray plant with systemic insecticide.

Buying your plants

If you are unable to raise your own plants from seed owing to lack of time or facilities you will still be able to buy, ready-to-plant, any of the subjects listed in this book. The best possible advice must be to purchase from a reliable nurseryman who has propagated and nurtured them from the start; failing this it is possible to buy from garden centres, superstores, florists, greengrocers and even ironmongers. Some of these may not be suitably equipped to look after living plants so purchase with care.

Look for healthy and sturdy plants, not far advanced in flower. Make sure that the variety is the correct one for the container you have in mind. A 4ft (1m) dahlia will look a little odd in a windowbox. You are unlikely to need many plants and it will be worth the extra small cost to buy single plants, container-grown, rather than a box of fifty, half of which you will probably throw away. A good nurseryman will be choosing most of his seed from the more expensive F.1. seed lists and he is more likely to be growing these in containers than crowded in a seed tray, which is another good reason for the selection of this type.

Examine evergreens for the presence of scale insects. Yellow leaves on any plant indicate neglect at some stage of growth. If the plant has a flower at time of purchase you will be certain it is the one you wanted but don't get carried away by one that is in full bloom. It may look good but won't last.

Buying seed: F.1 hybrid seed is produced by crossing two varieties, each with desired characteristics. It is expensive but results more than compensate for this in vigour, plant habit and flower production. Always try to buy in foil sealed packs; once opened, seed will begin to deteriorate gradually so do not open until ready to sow. Seed in colourful paper packets may look tempting but the seed inside may not live up to the printing so buy from a reliable source. Never buy seed packeted in paper from an outdoor vending stand as unless seed is sealed in an inner packet moisture absorbed by the packet may have started the process of germination.

Acknowledgements

Colour artwork by Bob Bampton and Andrew Riley/The Garden Studio and Jane Pickering/Linden Artists
Line artwork by Norman Bancroft-Hunt (pp. 6-7) and Patricia Newton
Photographs by The Harry Smith Horticultural Photographic Collection and David Cockroft
Designed by Marion Neville
Typeset by Faz Graphics Ltd